AMERICAN

HERITAGE

October 1958 · Volume IX, Number 6

Cheyenne Brothers Starting On A Hunt

Cheyenne Brothers Returning From A Hunt

PAINTINGS BY GEORGE CATLIN (1796-1872), AMERICAN MUSEUM OF NATURAL HISTORY

AMERICAN HERITAGE

The Magazine of History

PUBLISHER
James Parton

EDITORIAL DIRECTOR
Joseph J. Thorndike, Jr.

EDITOR
Bruce Catton

MANAGING EDITOR
Oliver Jensen

ASSOCIATE EDITORS
Richard M. Ketchum
Joan Paterson Mills

ASSISTANT EDITOR
Robert L. Reynolds

EDITORIAL ASSISTANTS
Hilde Heun, Stephen W. Sears
Caroline Backlund, Lilyan Goldman
Helen M. Brown, Robert Cowley
Beverly Hill

ART DIRECTOR
Irwin Glusker

ASSOCIATE ART DIRECTOR: Murray Belsky
ASSISTANT: Trudy Glucksberg
STAFF PHOTOGRAPHER: Herbert Loebel

ADVISORY BOARD
Allan Nevins, *Chairman*
Ray A. Billington   Louis C. Jones
Carl Carmer   Richard P. McCormick
Albert B. Corey   Harry Shaw Newman
Christopher Crittenden Howard H. Peckham
Marshall B. Davidson   S. K. Stevens
Arthur M. Schlesinger, Sr.

CIRCULATION DIRECTOR
Richard V. Benson

AMERICAN HERITAGE is published every two months by American Heritage Publishing Co., Inc., 551 Fifth Avenue, New York 17, N. Y.
Single Copies: $2.95
Annual Subscriptions: $12.50 in the U.S.A.
$13.50 elsewhere

An annual Index of AMERICAN HERITAGE is published every February, priced at $1.00. AMERICAN HERITAGE is also indexed in *Readers' Guide to Periodical Literature.*

Application for Second-Class mail privileges is pending at New York, N. Y.

Sponsored by

American Association for State & Local History · Society of American Historians

CONTENTS *October 1958 · Volume IX, Number 6*

COVER: Two years after John Rolfe married "an unbeleeving creature, namely, Pokahuntas," in newly founded Virginia, he took his Indian bride back to England; there this portrait was painted by an unknown artist in 1616. Pocahontas (also known as Matoaka, and by her baptismal name of Rebecca) is appealing in stiff, confining Stuart garb, but she scarcely suggests the child of nature who danced naked before Captain John Smith in far-off America (see page 28). The painting now hangs in the National Gallery of Art in Washington. *Back Cover:* A Miss Betsey Woods executed this typical female seminary water color sometime during the nineteenth century; it is now in the New York State Historical Association folk art collection at Cooperstown. The Peeping Tom in the bushes is trying to decipher a note that reads rather primly: "Either in joy or sorrow my friend shall participate in my feelings."

Patrolling the Middle

brutal and cunning slave trade, but Southern influenc

J. M. W. Turner's well-known painting, Slavers Throwing Overboard the Dead and Dying, *was exhibited in 1840 and moved the*

Passage

Congress agreed to join Britain in suppressing the

hamstrung the Navy when it came to enforcing the law

By J. C. FURNAS

novelist Thackeray to write: "Ye gods, what a 'middle passage'."

The American merchantman *Mary Ann* was primly named, but she had a scandalous history. In 1848 she cleared for West Africa, ostensibly on a trading voyage for such products as palm oil, which the new American railroads and factories used as a lubricant. Her mates and crew seemed to have signed on unaware that any other scheme was in the wind. But the course her captain set took her not to the mouths of the Niger, focus of the palm oil trade, but to the Gallinas River area, notorious for its bootleg slave markets.

Forty years before, Great Britain and the United States had outlawed the slave trade, and eventually the whole western world followed suit. Subsequently the United States had declared slave trading to be piracy, subject to capital punishment. But booms in sugar and coffee kept Cuba and Brazil hungry for slave labor, and immense profits from slave smuggling brought unscrupulous seamen and shipowners—"the matured villainy of the world," a U.S. Navy commander called them—flocking like buzzards into a rich racket.

The captain of the *Mary Ann* was one of these. But his crewmen were not, and at the sight of the dismal Gallinas shore they decided they wanted no part whatever in the skipper's plans. So, taking things into their own hands, they put him ashore and sailed off down the coast looking for a U.S. Navy vessel to which they could surrender. Finding none, they took the *Mary Ann* back to New York, turned her over to the federal authorities—and promptly found themselves in serious trouble. From one point of view they had most commendably refused to become accessories to the foulest of seagoing crimes. But from another, they had committed mutiny, perhaps barratry, and a few other odd maritime sins. The court held that there had been "probable cause" for the arrest of the *Mary Ann* as a slaver, but it was lenient with the members of the crew, and let them off with no heavier penalty than forfeiture of their wages for both outward and homeward voyages. Considering the innocence of their motives, the penalty seems heavy enough.

Now contrast this with the history of another American ship, the *Rebecca*, also primly named, also West

Africa-bound on an ostensibly legitimate voyage in 1859. She was a Baltimore-built clipper of a design renowned for speed, and she was transporting forty-odd freed Negroes from New Orleans to settle in Liberia; from there she was to continue to the Congo River with two Spanish traders and their stocks of goods. Nearing Liberia she was overhauled by the steamer H.M.S. *Viper,* a small British man-of-war on antislaving duty. The *Viper's* commander, apparently well aware that the *Rebecca* enjoyed a dubious reputation, was much annoyed to find her on so innocent a mission, but he allowed her to proceed. She duly landed the emigrants and their belongings and then, once at sea again, she assumed her true character—that of a slaver procuring Negroes for the great, quasi-official slave market in Cuba.

Her real owners were not the New Orleans firm that had registered her as American, but the two Spanish "passengers." They had sought this Liberian errand as a way to secure unimpeachable clearance papers, and they now took over as captain and supercargo. They mustered the crew and signed the ship's company to new articles at wages eloquent of how well slave bootlegging paid: captain and mate were to receive $5,000 each for the voyage; second mate, $3,500; carpenter, $3,000; seamen, $1,500 each—this at a time when a dollar bought six or seven times what it does now.

After some mischances and delays, the *Rebecca* entered the Congo to size up the situation and, if possible, to get "slaved." Just at that most inopportune moment, H.M.S. *Tigris,* another British patrol ship, apparently also well alerted, came prowling along and set an armed boat's crew to keep round-the-clock watch on the *Rebecca.* Then appeared a Portuguese cruiser—even less welcome because, whereas the Brit-

ish usually turned slaver crews loose after confiscating the ships, the Portuguese had lately developed a nasty habit of sending slavers to their rugged penal colonies. H.M.S. *Vixen* (a third Britisher) and the fast-sailing U.S.S. *Vincennes* were also rumored to be in the vicinity. There were altogether too many men-of-war thereabouts, and sulkily the *Rebecca* dropped down the river still un-"slaved," let the hovering *Tigris* know that trade had been poor and that she was returning stateside disconsolate—and ostentatiously put to sea on a northwesterly course.

When she was well over the horizon her Spanish commander had her hove to, stripped of all identifying marks, and further disguised with a coat of black paint. He then sailed back, landing well south of the Congo to get "slaved" quickly and away. It was a calculated risk, but it paid off. In a short time the *Rebecca* had taken aboard almost 1,200 Negroes, mostly men and boys, who would fetch perhaps $400,000 at Cuban prices. Just as the last few were coming on board, the *Vixen* hove in sight. As the *Rebecca* hastily weighed anchor, the *Vixen,* finding her warning shots ignored, opened fire in earnest at long range. But her gunnery was not all it might have been. The *Rebecca* got to sea unscathed and, thanks to her Baltimore breeding, soon showed her heels to the puffing little teakettle.

The homeward voyage was uneventful. The slaves were landed on a small island off the south coast of Cuba to be shifted a few at a time to mainland plantations. The beautiful clipper was scuttled and burned so as to leave no trace of these doings, and her crew went their separate ways with bulging pockets. Even after paying them off and destroying a valuable 550-ton ship, the *Rebecca's* owners probably netted $150,-

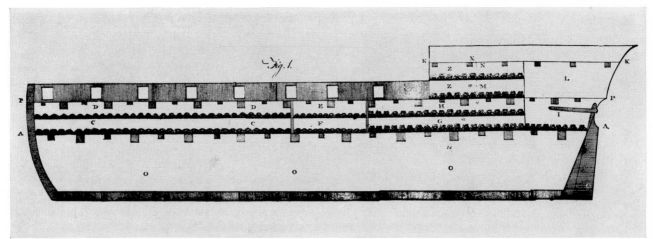

The prints of the plan (above) *and section* (opposite) *of the slave ship* Brookes, *from Thomas Clarkson's 1808* History of the Abolition of the African Slave Trade, *were used by a British parliamentary committee to dramatize the slaves' suffering.*

ooo on the voyage, the equivalent of three-quarters of a million dollars today.

Between them, the caper of the *Rebecca*—carried out under the Stars and Stripes—and that ironical miscarriage of justice in the *Mary Ann* case point up two curious, interconnected scandals that were at their ripest a hundred years ago: the genius of American shore authorities for making the antislaving laws look foolish, and the U.S. Navy's poor record in bringing slave ships to book.

Neither the *Rebecca* nor the *Mary Ann* sighted an American man-of-war; even when she tried hard, the *Mary Ann* hadn't been able to find one. The reasons were that, at the time, the U.S. African squadron had only five ships and that nobody in Washington really wanted them to prove much anyway.

The Navy's poor showing was more the fault of politicians than of commodores. In 1842, six years before the *Mary Ann* affair, the United States had formally agreed with Britain that each should maintain off the West African coast an antislaving squadron mounting a total of at least eighty guns. Regularly spurred by zealous antislavery cabinet ministers, the British Navy, except during the short naval emergency of the Crimean War, always assigned ships far in excess of this requirement. The American squadron, on the other hand, was seldom much above quota and often fell well below it. Number of ships, not of guns, was the crucial thing, anyway. Relying mostly on speed and guile, slavers seldom tried to shoot it out. When overhauled they would knuckle under to an 8-gun schooner as readily as to a 44-gun frigate, and ten small vessels could patrol five times as much coast as could the two frigates that would answer the gun requirement. The British Navy, which meant business, used such small men-of-war on this duty, their

squadron averaging eighteen vessels in the period 1842-57. The squadron of the U.S. Navy averaged four.

The treaty would have been more effective, too, had it stipulated the number of ships actually on patrol. The British got much time-on-the-job out of theirs by basing them at Sierra Leone, next door to the Gallinas, or on the island of Fernando Po, just off the concentrated slaving nests of the African coast. The U.S. squadron was based in the Cape Verde Islands, 2,000-odd miles from the Congo, 800 from the Gallinas. More than half the time, the American ships were refitting in port or voyaging between base and station. In the mid-1840's the United States brig *Truxtun*, for instance, though she sailed under an unusually brisk commander, spent only 181 days cruising on station out of a total West African hitch of 468 days.

The most illustrious ships of the old Navy—*Constitution, Constellation, United States, Macedonian*—and a good number of famous Navy officers served in the African squadron. Names on the old dispatches from West Africa include Matthew Calbraith Perry, who opened up Japan, and enjoyed neither of his two West African commands; Josiah Tatnall, who told the British commodore that "Blood is thicker than water"; Andrew H. Foote, whose gunboats on the western waters were to do so much to destroy the Confederacy. It was Foote, in a book written in the early 1850's, who protested vigorously against the unnecessary restrictions imposed on commanders on the African station, and he spoke for many of his fellow officers.

The basic cause of their frustration was the South's growing reluctance to see any aspect of slavery damaged, at home or abroad. Southern Congressmen encouraged the Navy Department to drag its feet. Orders made it clear that the African squadron's first concern

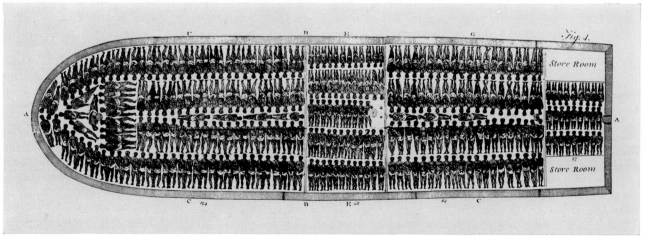

The parliamentary committee estimated that 450 slaves of all ages could be carried on this ship, whose lower deck was 100 feet long and 25 feet wide. But it was later proved that the Brookes *had carried as many as 609 slaves on a single voyage.*

was not hunting slavers but protecting the American-sponsored colony of Liberia for free Negroes and the growing American-West African trade. Ships were often ordered home long before their replacements, sailing tardily from Brooklyn or Boston, could possibly arrive. Almost as soon as steam took to sea the British were sending to West Africa steam-propelled men-of-war which, while they might fall behind the slaver's clippers in a brisk and steady wind, could overhaul even the fastest fugitive in calm or uncertain air. Not until shortly before the Civil War did U.S. Navy steamers appear off West Africa, although American officers repeatedly asked for them. One conscientious commodore reported in 1860 that "the African squadron, under my command, has done its whole duty"; but he went on bitterly: ". . . this has been done in the face of positive discouragement from the Department." In the mid-1840's West African service under a less active American commodore had moved a young lieutenant to call the whole operation "sending a squadron of gallant ships to chase shadows in a deadly climate."

His complaint about the climate was only partly justified. Yellow fever, malaria, and odd enteric diseases made the West African shore deadly enough to whites, and small British ships blockading slaving nests close inshore or sending boats' crews up the rivers often lost many men. But U.S. Navy ships usually patrolled well out at sea, far enough to minimize the risk from disease-carrying mosquitoes. The shadow-chasing charge, however, was valid: it was a disgusted tribute to the skill with which slavers exploited Uncle Sam's wrongheaded refusal either to fish or to cut bait.

Britain had tried hard to quicken the U.S. government's lagging steps. After 1808 she had used diplomacy, cash payments, and force to persuade each maritime nation that had outlawed the slave trade to sign with her a treaty of "reciprocal search and seizure" to help enforce the antislaving declarations. Under these treaties the British Navy acquired the right to board Nation A's ships at sea and, if evidence of slaving were found, to seize them and send them into port for legal penalties. Nation A's navy had the same right with regard to British ships. But after Trafalgar the British Navy became and remained so much larger than any other and Britain's successive governments were so severe toward the slave trade that in effect this system of treaties pretty well turned over to England the job of suppressing the slave trade on the high seas.

By 1840 she had signed up all the major maritime powers—except the United States. We held out because we were still smarting from the British Navy's highhanded visit-and-search procedures during the Napoleonic Wars; indeed, these had constituted one of the most inflammatory causes of the miserable little War of 1812. The United States always fell back on the contention that each nation should skin its own skunks, that ships on lawful errands flying the American flag as a token of American registry should be examined only by U.S. Navy vessels, that we could take care of our own slavers and prevent abuse of our own flag—let other nations do the same with theirs. Yet it was obvious that the U.S. Navy, much smaller than Britain's, probably lacked the resources, and that the federal government certainly lacked the real desire, to do anything of the sort.

The case of the *Rebecca* illustrates how the consequent racket worked: By the late 1840's, the typical slaver was a big, fast, stateside-built ship with a few Yankees among a mixed crew of foreign skimmings (the *Rebecca* had Turks, Scots, Greeks, Danes, Italians, and Spaniards). The slaver indulged in games of tag with antislaving patrol ships, usually British, using her United States registry as a mask for actual Latin-American ownership represented by men who were nominally "passengers," and having Cuba as destination and market. It was not quite typical of her period, however, that the *Rebecca* hailed from New Orleans. Slavers occasionally did come from there or from Boston, Salem, Portland, or Philadelphia. But more and more New York came to dominate this crass industry, furnishing the ships, the men to navigate them, the goods to swap for slaves—and, as time passed, New York interests put up ever larger amounts of minority capital, well hidden under layers of subterfuge. In the twenty months ending August, 1860, a good hundred slavers were known to have fitted out in and sailed from New York Harbor.

United States registry, combined with a set of bogus Spanish or Portuguese papers easily obtainable by bribery, was the basic dodge. If the ship were challenged by a U.S. Navy cruiser, she hoisted Spanish colors, say, and the Spanish "passenger," temporarily turned captain, showed the Spanish papers to the boarding party, while the American captain stayed out of sight. Such subterfuges were so rife in the 1840's that a U.S. commodore reported that the American flag had completely disappeared from West African slaving—though the whole seagoing world knew that the waters off West Africa were swarming with slavers that freely hoisted the Stars and Stripes whenever it suited their needs and a U.S. Navy vessel was not around. For if the cruiser were British, the slaver hoisted American colors, and could usually count on being left unmolested. In the absence of a search-and-seizure treaty British Navy commanders had been or-

Less successful than many of her sister slavers, the American barque Orion *was overhauled and captured in 1859 by H.M.S.* Pluto. *The* Pluto *was typical of the steam ships that gradually replaced sailing vessels in the British antislaving squadron.*

dered not to meddle with American ships unless they were quite confident they could be proved to be slavers—when, for instance, the cruiser had picked up the festering stench that usually betrayed the presence of a closely-packed human cargo.

To reduce the advantage that American mulishness thus gave to slavers, the British inserted the so-called equipment clause in their antislaving treaties. Originally a slaver could be apprehended only when slaves were actually found on board. But by the mid-1830's Britain was seizing ships which, even though they were carrying no slaves, had on board most of the equipment slaving required: extra-wide hatchways fitted with gratings (for ventilation of slave quarters); more rice or casks of fresh water than the ship's crew could conceivably need; unduly ample cooking facilities. Even American courts, usually lackadaisical or worse about slaving cases, came to condemn solely on such circumstantial evidence if it were strong enough.

The slavers responded with even more involved jugglings of flags and papers to forestall search, sometimes using as many as four "captains" of different nationalities, each of whom had papers to match. The grim nature of their commerce makes it good to know that every now and then they overplayed their shabby hand or guessed wrong and came to grief. In 1839, for instance, the Baltimore-built slaver *Catharine,* owned by Havana interests, was nearing West Africa

when she fell in with and was chased by H.M.S. *Dolphin.* Unable to outdistance her pursuer after two hours, she played the usual card and hoisted American colors. But the British commander, for some reason very sure of her character, took a chance and opened fire. Hove to and searched, the *Catharine* proved to have on board cooking arrangements for 300 people; planks marked and numbered for speedy building of a half-deck for slaves; 570 wooden spoons and about 350 pairs of handcuffs. On the American captain's person were found written instructions advising him how to persuade boarding officers that his Spanish and Portuguese shipmates were passengers and that his handful of American seamen constituted the entire crew. He was even keeping one log in English, another in Spanish. It was ingenious but futile. A British prize crew took the ship to New York, where she was duly condemned.

One of the most elaborate ruses of all was undertaken by Captain Cyrus Libby of Maine, master of the American-built brig *Porpoise.* The *Porpoise* had made several slaving voyages under the ownership of certain Brazilians but was prepared whenever necessary to show American colors, papers, captain, and crew. On her last voyage, however, she merely acted as tender for the American-built *Kentucky,* which actually loaded the Negroes. The *Porpoise*'s job was to transport to the slaving point a Brazilian captain-super-

CONTINUED ON PAGE 101

DAYLIGHT in the SWAMP

Old-time logging in the Pacific Northwest was "a wildly wonderful if tragically heedless era"; there are those who still mourn its passing

By STEWART H. HOLBROOK

The tradition of the American lumberjack is an ancient one, as industrial antiquity goes in the United States. It began more than three hundred years ago, some say in 1631, when colonists set up the first sawmill in America in what is now South Berwick, Maine, and fed it with the great white pines, a classic species whose graceful outline was soon to appear on flags, provincial coats of arms, even on shillings.

It was here in the New England timber, too, that certain customs and practices originated which were to follow the loggers across the continent. For instance, an early timber baron was Sir William Pepperell, who, says an old memoir, appeared at his log landings along the Saco River "attired in a coat of scarlet cloth." This is the earliest record of brilliant garb worn in connection with logging, and one likes to think it was from Sir William that the lumberjack took his liking for red, whether of sash, shirt, or honest woolen underwear.

Logging Days: A Special Portfolio

In the late 1880's a Missourian named Darius Kinsey (right) arrived in Seattle, the raucous, mushrooming metropolis of the Pacific Northwest. The logging industry was enjoying a spectacular growth; simultaneously, photography was just becoming popular. In this meeting of historical circumstances "Dee" Kinsey found his future and his fame. Within a few years he began earning his livelihood by trekking into the tall timber, photographing loggers (left) as they felled the giant trees, and then selling them prints for fifty cents apiece. "You aren't a logger," he would tell them, "until you own a dollar watch and have your picture taken with a tree." For Kinsey, a small man physi-cally, the work was laborious. His cam-eras were primitive and cumbersome. He had to pack his exposed glass plates in wooden boxes and ship them to his home. There they were processed by Mrs. Kinsey and the children, who sent the prints back to him for distribution. His mobile workshop—at first a horse-drawn wagon and later the car shown behind him at right in 1914—was a fa-miliar sight around logging camps for nearly half a century until he retired in 1940 at 69. The photographs on these and the next eight pages—owned by Jesse E. Ebert and obtained for AMERI-CAN HERITAGE by Jay Culver of Culver Service—are part of Kinsey's unique visual record of logging's halcyon days.

There was also the attempt of the Crown to prevent the loggers from cutting every tree that grew. The Royal Navy wanted the best trees saved for masts, but the attempt to reserve them was futile. Neither the royal taboo mark of the Broad Arrow on the finest timber nor penalties as severe as those against heresy could stop the red-shirted boys from cutting everything that stood in their way. Their persistence survived down to our own time.

Meanwhile, the isolation of logging camps, combined with an occupation so dangerous to life as to remove all but the toughest and most alert, conspired to produce a unique race of men whose dedicated goal was to let daylight into the swamp and thus, as they saw it, permit the advance of civilization. For generations the customary getting-up cry in camp was "Daylight in the swamp—all out!"

When the Yankee loggers had cleared the white pines, the main body of them moved to join their kind in New York and Pennsylvania, where more pine and then the spruce and the hemlock went down before them like so much wheat in a storm. They did not stop. Before the Civil War they were letting daylight into the swamps around Saginaw Bay in Michigan, and when they had mowed their way across that state they tied into Wisconsin. Here in the lake states they began to discard the slow oxen in favor of horses; their steam-driven sawmills meantime were growing in size and speed and responding to native ingenuity. When cold weather froze the log ponds, they no longer sat around waiting for spring: some genius ran a steampipe into the frozen pond, thawed it, and sawed boards all winter. They discarded the old circular saw and replaced it with a bright, thin band of glittering teeth that wailed like a banshee as it made boards to build Midwestern cities and sawdust piles so high they could be seen decades later. In both mills and woods they bent every effort to get more speed—speed to cut the timber which they believed would last a hundred years, if not forever.

The Michigan and Wisconsin timber did not last forever, so the boys tore into Minnesota like locusts, and like locusts took all before them. What they did not cut they and the settlers managed to set afire, creating some of the most horrible disasters imagi-

TEXT CONTINUED ON PAGE 77
PORTFOLIO OF ILLUSTRATIONS CONTINUED ON OPPOSITE PAGE

Two high riggers, *far up on the trunk, attach lines to a spar tree. To the spar, focal point for high-lead logging, were attached one or more block-and-tackle mechanisms; with the aid of cables and a steam-powered donkey engine (in the shed at left), the biggest logs could be hauled out of the woods to the railhead. Today, donkeys are diesel-powered, but the high-lead is still the chief method of yarding logs.*

Before commercial railroads came to the tall timber, loggers built "trailing railroads" on which strings of logs were dragged between the rails. This was the five-mile line of the Forks Logging Company at Monroe, Washington. On a single trip the 45-ton Climax locomotive dragged a dozen 32- to 40-foot logs to the Snohomish River to be floated to the mill. In one year 40,000,000 board feet of timber traveled over this line.

The Vanzer family posed for Kinsey outside their home in the Washington wilderness in 1906. The outhouse, crudely roofed over with boards, is under the raised tree roots at far left. Homesteaders like Vanzer, called "stumpranchers," worked all week in a logging camp or a sawmill and had only Sundays at home. Kinsey was an early advocate of natural-light photography and, as the sharp details here show, he achieved amazing clarity.

A falling-crew rests after undercutting a ten-foot-thick fir. Standing on springboards inserted into the trunk, they hacked away with double-bitted axes, placing the cut so the tree would fall where they wanted it to, then finished the job with a two-man saw and wedges. The bottle at left holds saw oil; the other, water.

Kinsey photographed all 34 crew members of one logging "side," or location, in 1908, seated on huge fir logs at a loading works. A line horse and donkey engine are at the extreme left. In the background at left, a Shay locomotive with steam up waits to move the rear log, already loaded on a car, away from the deck, or landing.

Left: After the fallers brought down the tree, a bucker cut it into manageable lengths. This bucker is about to start on a twelve-foot-thick cedar. His was a dangerous job; for a log, as it parted from the trunk, could roll over and crush him. Kinsey, feeling that accidents discredited logging, almost never photographed them.

Much Pacific Northwest timber grew in rugged, mountainous country, and to span the deep canyons and ravines logging railroaders had to build their own trestles. Sometimes, as shown in the photograph above taken by Kinsey in 1900, they underestimated the stresses or overloaded their trains, and then bridge, engine, cars, and logs all came tumbling down. But in other cases, like the 893-foot trestle at right, 203 feet above Cedar River Canyon, Washington, they accomplished remarkable works of engineering marked by a primitive grandeur.

On the preceding page: One of Darius Kinsey's most famous photographs, taken in 1892 near Arlington, Washington, recalls Northwest logging's pioneer days. Before the coming of donkey engines and railroads, timber was hauled out by powerful bull teams over a skid road of half-buried logs. Here a team of twelve, driven by a hard-bitten bullwhacker (right foreground), start a turn of logs to the mill. Logs were barked to ease their passage, and often a boy went ahead of the logs to oil the skids. "Of all the types of power brought into the timber," an old logger said, "only the bull teams served man's stomach. The accident victims could be eaten. The loudest cuss ever heard in a bunkhouse was when a logger bit into a yoke buckle in his beef roast."

MR. GODEY'S LADY

Gentle Sarah Hale, widowed at forty, created our first successful women's

magazine and popularized the Paris fashions she regarded with deep distrust

By RALPH NADING HILL

Mention the words "women's rights" and much the same picture storms into the average American recollection: the grim-lipped, podium-pounding suffragette of the late nineteenth century. She has three resonant names (very likely one of them is Carrie) and you cannot by the wildest stretch of the imagination conjure up an image of her reading nursery rhymes to the young. Is not the gap between social reform and "Mary Had A Little Lamb" too wide and too dramatic to bridge?

In fact, it is not. For the lady who invented Mary in 1830 and saw her pass into folklore via McGuffey's *Readers* probably had more influence on women's status than her noisier sisters. Her name was Sarah Josepha Hale, and as editor of *Godey's Lady's Book* for forty years, she set a pattern for today's women's magazines and deeply influenced two generations of American wives and mothers in her own lifetime.

Her reward, of course, has been to be generally forgotten, both for the rhyme and for the remarkable career. Her magazine has been replaced by a flossier product aimed at a much more sophisticated, if not really happier, audience than the huge one that for decades looked to Mrs. Hale for advice on fashions, homemaking, health, and child-rearing. The old *Lady's Books,* where they survive, are to be found in old-fashioned at-

tics, themselves rapidly vanishing under the assault of a kind of residential architecture that Mrs. Hale would have disliked immensely.

Sarah Hale seems, at first blush, to have been a perfect contradiction, not only in her looks and actions but in what she said and did. A wholesome, soft-spoken mother of five children, she was the antithesis of the seriocomic suffragette. With a clear conscience Mrs. Hale could announce that "the most important vocation on earth is that of the Christian mother in her nursery," and at the same time be leading campaigns for women doctors, nurses, professors, missionaries, sales clerks, and waiters. The editor of a magazine for elegant women, she could decry the wasp waist and drive her readers out of their parlors into the sunshine (but not—Heaven forbid! —in bloomers).

She was born Sarah Buell on a farm near the little village of Newport, New Hampshire, in 1788. Schools for girls were almost unheard of in those days, and young Sarah received her early education from reading the Bible and the English classics; from the instruction of her mother, whom she remembered as a woman with "a mind clear as rock-water"; and later from an older brother who went to Dartmouth. On the strength of these attainments, she started a small private school when she was only eighteen and kept it

GODEY'S "AMERICANISED" PARIS FASHIONS.

Sarah Josepha Hale had been editor of Godey's Lady's Book *for thirteen years when this picture of her appeared in the December, 1850, issue with some warm words from her publisher, Louis A. Godey (right). "A portrait without a biography is a novelty," wrote Godey, "but Mrs. Hale insists. She is one of the most sensible and energetic of all the conductors of the numerous magazines now published."*

for several years. Then, in 1811, David Hale, a young lawyer, opened an office in Newport, and two years later he and Sarah Buell were married.

It was a happy marriage, and one which had a good deal to do with Mrs. Hale's subsequent career. Though new members of the family started putting in their appearance almost at once, their arrival did not extinguish the young housewife's intellectual interests. One day a friend dropped in with a new book, and Mrs. Hale, who had been in the midst of cleaning house, put aside her broom and read on for hours. In the evenings she and her husband studied together, for regular two-hour periods, subjects like French, botany, and geology. David Hale seems also to have encouraged his wife to write articles and stories for local newspapers; some time later, in a brief autobiographical note, she remembered with gratitude that he had helped direct her away from the pompous, rhetorical prose style characteristic of the time.

And then in 1822, suddenly, "as with a stroke," David Hale died, a few days before the birth of their fifth child, leaving his widow with very little in the way of material resources. With the help of his Masonic friends, Sarah Hale and her sister-in-law tried the millinery business for a while, but her mind and heart weren't in it. She had written a few poems, and these, plus her first novel, *Northwood, A Tale of New England,* published in 1827, brought her to the attention of the Reverend John Lauris Blake, an Episcopal clergyman in Boston who wanted to start a women's magazine. He offered Mrs. Hale the editorship, and despite the warnings of her friends, she accepted.

The warnings were based on hard economic facts. Many women's magazines had bloomed and as quickly faded. Advertising, the bread and butter of most mod-

ern magazines, was in its infancy; not until the 1870's would it become a prime factor in publishing success. In addition, no one knew for certain how big the audience for a women's magazine might be, and no one had succeeded in achieving the right editorial balance to keep that audience interested.

Mrs. Hale thought she knew the combination. Her predecessors in the field had, according to a biographer, Lawrence Martin, writing in *The New England Quarterly,* "dedicated themselves to fashion and pleasure and a gentle dalliance and frivolity that never trespassed morally." Mrs. Hale's pages, by contrast, were to be "consecrated to duty and domesticity, and the preparation of woman for a larger and more serious sphere." She saw her public, Martin continues, as

an untapped and as yet inarticulate group of Mrs. Hales—middle-class women; women of the sewing circle rather than of the salon, and of the lyceum rather than of the theater; women coping with life on serious terms, earnest about philanthropies and progress, proud of their new country, busily endowing the old-fashioned religion with a new outlook—not the pampered and over-leisured dolls of Boston and provincial parlors, but leaners upon domestic broomsticks and supporters of books; women interested in extramural activities but for intra-mural ends.

When in 1828 she moved her family to Boston and entered upon the national stage as the editor of the *Ladies' Magazine,* Mrs. Hale was a woman of forty, just under middle height, with a fair, pink-and-white complexion, sparkling hazel eyes, and brown hair which she continued to wear in the side-curls her husband had so much admired. She dressed conservatively but was always exquisitely groomed; she walked briskly and carried herself very erect, and this, in combination with the full, sweeping skirts of the day,

TEXT CONTINUED ON PAGE 97

A PORTFOLIO OF ILLUSTRATIONS BEGINS ON THE OPPOSITE PAGE

IDEAS TO INTEREST EVERY WOMAN

Samples of "The Work Table" (right) are evidence of Mrs. Hale's early interest in female do-it-yourself. In addition to items like the Greek smoking cap (undoubtedly for the man who had everything), and complicated headdresses (below) to be whipped up without resort to the local beauty parlor, she included an intriguing column called (in the old Yankee spelling) "New Receipts." One issue devoted this space to telling the lady of the house how "to remove the black dye left on the skin from wearing mourning in warm weather. . . . No family should be without it." Godey's Model Cottages were a standard feature and the Tudor example here could be built for $3,200 in 1851. The elaborate dressing tables and cradles served as hints on how to decorate them.

THE WORK TABLE.

COVER FOR TASSEL OF WINDOW-BLIND   EMBROIDERY.—GREEK SMOKING CAP.

LATEST FASHION FOR HEAD-DRESSES

[FRONT VIEW.]

[BACK VIEW.]

TOILET TABLES.

CRADLES

"ONE BLAZE OF BEAUTY"

Typical of the bathos that brimmed in Godey's *are The Dress-Maker and The Dress-Wearer (left) illustrating a December, 1851, story. Under them James Russell Lowell opened the tear ducts with the following lines:*

> Hark! that rustle of a dress,
> Stiff with lavish costliness!
> Here comes one whose cheek would flush
> But to have her garments brush
> 'Gainst the girl whose fingers thin
> Wove the weary 'broidery in. . . .

At right and below are examples from the thirties and forties of the famous fashion plates that were often cut out and framed with loving care. A decade later Godey's *boasted that its "reliable fashion plates will be under the sole superintendence of a lady who receives proof sheets of the fashions direct from Paris. . . . We have so long led in this department that the fact would hardly be worth mentioning, excepting that others claim the merit that has so long been conceded to the 'Book.' They will be got up, as usual, in our superior style to the French." Thus, dispensing with competitors and originators in rapid order, Publisher Godey continued for the rest of his lifetime to spend money lavishly on the hand-colored plates that made* Godey's Lady's Book, *in his own words, "one blaze of beauty throughout."*

MRS. HALE BELIEVED IN BEING HEARTY

Whereas fashion for his "fair ladies" came first in Godey's favor, Mrs. Hale counterbalanced the harmful effects with an illustrated section on "Health and Beauty." This ran the gamut from how to just plain walk or exercise with "scepters" (below) to the rigorous calisthenics shown above and airily disposed of as a "gentler sort of gymnastics suited to girls." Archery was also deemed a suitable path to health and beauty, but the odds-on favorite was equestrianism for the fair sex and pictures of pretty riders were plentiful. As the doctor who edited this section pointed out, "It would be a prejudicial error to suppose that females should be subjected only to passive exercises."

THE SLOW WALK, OR MARCH.   THE QUICK PACE.

Fig. 1.   Fig. 2.   Fig. 3.

Fig. 4.   Fig. 5.   Fig. 6.

This portrait of John Smith was made by Simon de Passe, one of the foremost engravers of his day, for Smith's map of New England. The map, with the places named by Prince Charles himself, appeared in A Description of New England, *written while Smith was a prisoner of pirates who had captured him on his second trip to New England.*

WAS JOHN SMITH A LIAR?

One lady, he said, saved his head from the block; now

another is rescuing his reputation   *By* MARSHALL FISHWICK

John Smith is one of those persons about whom historians are apt to lose their tempers.   JOHN FISKE

Standing on the threshold of American history is one of its most colorful and controversial figures, Captain John Smith. Although he spent only a few years in America—at Jamestown, the first permanent English settlement on the continent —he became one of its first heroes. But for three and a half centuries his reputation has struggled through seas as stormy as those on which his tiny ships wallowed. His fame, which rests on his own extensive accounts, has been attacked from all directions—by his contemporaries and by scholars and historians of succeeding generations. Was John Smith a liar? Or was his own dramatic story of his life the simple truth? The writer bold enough to put forth an answer would do well to have a sword as well as a typewriter around, for in our time, as in 1607, the very name John Smith can cause blood pressures to rise.

The origin of the controversy is to be found in the tragedy and misery of the early Virginia years. It was natural that some settlers should try to fix the blame for their misfortunes, and that others should seek credit for the survival of the colony. Among the latter, hardly a single leader made a claim not hotly disputed by his companions, and later generations have taken sides just as dogmatically. Because Smith's claims were the most startling, they have been the most warmly attacked—and defended.

To begin with, he claimed that even before coming to the New World he had accomplished deeds of derring-do against Europe's age-old enemies, the Turks. As a volunteer with the Austrian forces on the Hungarian and Transylvanian border, he had, he alleged, beheaded three Turks in open combat, winning the title of captain and a coat of arms for his trouble. Subsequently, he had been enslaved; befriended in Turkey by "a noble gentlewoman of some claim"; and sent around the Black Sea before returning to England. At Jamestown a few years later, he claimed, he had assumed command of the struggling colony and saved it from starvation by obtaining food from the Indians. To crown it all there was his tale— one of the most appealing in early American history —of his last-minute rescue from death by the beautiful Indian princess Pocahontas.

But did the rescue actually take place? Did Pocahontas love Smith, and did she pine for him after his departure? Was he really the subjugator of "nine and thirty kings" in his Indian forays? Was he really Jamestown's savior, and were later American colonies actually, in his words, "pigs of my own sow," and, anteri-

The author is indebted to Dr. Laura Polanyi Striker, who did the basic research which this article follows in exploring John Smith's Hungarian years. Dr. Striker, who is the final authority on these years, is now at work on a detailed study of The Affaire Smith, *which will concentrate on its social and political implications.*

The illustrations from John Smith's True Travels *show him being thrown overboard by Pilgrims because he was a Protestant; signaling "Ebersbaught" for "Kissell" at Olumpaugh; and preparing the fire pots that raised the siege of Alba Regali.*

orly, what about those three decapitated Turks?

A few facts about John Smith are undisputed. He was born humbly in 1580, a son of a "poore tenant" who held farmland in Lincolnshire. At fifteen the boy was apprenticed to Thomas Sendall, a wealthy merchant. He found this too dull, and, after the death of his father in 1596, went abroad as a soldier of fortune, meeting his first action in the Low Countries. In 1601 he joined the Austrians as a volunteer against the Turks. Ferocious and merciless fighters who in the sixteenth century had threatened the very gates of Vienna, the Turks were generally regarded as the chief threat to European civilization. No wonder John Smith found in them suitable enemies.

Whatever his adventures in the wars, he returned to England in 1604. He was only 26 when the Virginia Company received its patent, but he so impressed the organizers that in spite of his lack of pedigree they sent him out in 1606 as a member of the resident council appointed by the company to manage the colony. En route he was imprisoned "because his name was mencioned in the intended and confessed mutiny." After his release, he explored the country and procured food for the famished colony. It was on one of these expeditions, Smith later related, that the Pocahontas incident took place.

Back at Jamestown he was again accused by his council enemies, this time on a charge based on the fact that he had lost two of his men to the Indians. He was sentenced to death, but on the eve of his execution, Captain Christopher Newport, who had been in command of the three ships that had brought the original colonists to Jamestown and who had subsequently gone back to England for supplies, returned and saved Smith's life.

Restored to grace, Smith led exploring parties to Chesapeake Bay and the Potomac and Rappahannock rivers. During the terrible winter of 1608, he assumed dictatorial powers and again managed to obtain from the Indians enough food to keep the Englishmen alive. Whether or not he saved the settlement, he certainly alienated most of its leaders. At one point, when Newport returned a second time with seventy settlers, among them a perfumer and six tailors, Smith, never one to keep his opinions to himself, penned a *Rude Reply* to his London superiors:

"When you send againe I entreat you rather send but thirty carpenters, husbandmen, gardiners, blacksmiths, masons, and diggers up of trees, roots, well provided, than a thousand of such as we have. For except we be able to lodge and feed them, the most will consume with want of necessaries before they can be made good for anything."

George Percy, youngest of the eight sons of the eighth Earl of Northumberland, thought Smith "ambityous, onworthy, and vayneglorious." Edward Maria Wingfield, aristocratic first president of the council in Virginia, claimed Smith had "told him playnly how he lied" about his adventures with the Indians, thus starting the interminable debate over the Captain's veracity. In the midst of all this wrangling, Smith was severely wounded by a gunpowder explosion and returned to England in October, 1609.

Surely he had been a key figure in the colony's beginning. But savior? There the quarrel begins.

About Smith no one seems to be neutral. His "ould soldiers" considered him a fearless commander, "whose adventures were our lives and whose losse, our deaths." After carefully studying Smith's works, Edward Arber, the scholarly nineteenth-century editor of Smith's works, stated he had "the character of a Gentleman and Officer." In addition to many authors' opinions, we have Smith's own work. Though his *True Relation of Occurrences and Accidents in Virginia* was published in 1608 (it did not mention his rescue by Pocahontas), most of Smith's accounts were written

three ſingle Combats before REGALL in TRANSILVANIA. His Encounter with TVRBASHAW Chap·7·

His Combat with GRVALGO. Capt of threehundred horſmen. Chap·7·

How he ſlew BONNY:MVLGRO. Chap·7·

The Hajdus in the besieged city of Regall challenged the Christians to individual combat to "please the ladies." John Smith volunteered, defeated two warriors, and then issued a challenge himself. It resulted in the death of a third eminent soldier.

when his days of exploration were over. After three shorter volumes, published in 1612, 1616, and 1620, he wrote his longest and most important work, *The Generall Historie of Virginia, New-England, and the Summer Isles* (1624). Here we find, for the first time, the Pocahontas story. Euphuistic and partisan, the book is nevertheless as accurate as those of most Elizabethan historians. Smith's historical reliability was generally accepted until after his death in 1631.

For years, American writers tended to take his romantic story as true. Noah Webster included it in eighteenth-century editions of *The Little Reader's Assistant.* "What a hero was Captain Smith! How many Turks and Indians did he slay!" Further proof of the national admiration for Smith came with the portrayal of *Pocahontas Saving the Life of Captain John Smith* above the west door of the new Capitol rotunda in Washington. When the Knickerbocker poet James Kirke Paulding traveled through Virginia in 1817, he observed: "Fortitude, valor, perseverance, industry, and little Pocahontas were their tutelary deities." What if the editor of the *North American Review,* in July, 1822, made light of Smith, who "challenged a

whole army in his youth, and solaced his riper years in the arms of the renowned Pocahontas"? Yankee jealousy, that was all.

Plays like J. N. Barker's *The Indian Princess,* Robert Owen's *Pocahontas,* and John Brougham's *Po-ca-hon-tas, Or the Gentle Savage* emphasized her dramatic rescue of Captain Smith. So did scores of "Indian" poems in ante-bellum journals. By 1850 the traditional picture of John Smith as savior of the Virginia colony, and of Pocahontas as his rescuer at the execution block, had not been seriously challenged. If the Captain found his chief defenders in Dixie, he at least had few defamers in the area he himself had named New England, when he explored that region several years after his Jamestown adventures.

After the mid-nineteenth century a major attack on John Smith began to shape up. In his 1858 *History of New England,* John Gorham Palfrey was "haunted by incredulity" concerning some of the Captain's adventures. Charles Deane, Boston merchant and historian, looked further into the matter and decided that Smith was a notorious liar and braggart who had invented the story of his rescue by Pocahontas after the

After his victory, the three heads were paraded before the general's tent and Smith was honored and rewarded. Later, he was wounded, captured, and sold into slavery. The last illustration shows him killing his owner and escaping on his horse.

ree TVRKS heads in a banner giuen him for Armes. Chap·8·

ro he was preſented to Prince SIGISMVNDVS. Chap·8·

Capt SMITH led Captiue to the BASHAW of NALBRITS in TARTARIA. Chap·12·

Drub. man Smith Basham

Capt SMITH killeth the BASHAW of Nalbrits and on his horſe eſcapeth Chap·17·

London Printe by Iames Reeu

31

lapse of many years. None of Smith's contemporaries knew of the episode, which Deane concluded was a fabrication.

So matters stood when the Civil War broke out. During the bitter postwar years, an abler historian than Palfrey or Deane—Henry Adams—got into the controversy. Adams had just returned from studying in Germany and was anxious to display his new methodology. In an article on John Smith in the *North American Review* for January, 1867, he set down for textual comparison parallel passages from Smith's *A True Relation* and his *Generall Historie*. He found the Pocahontas rescue story spurious and labeled Smith incurably vain and incompetent. Adams thought the readiness with which Smith's version had been received less remarkable than "the credulity which has left it unquestioned almost to the present day." While the *Nation* doubted if "Mr. Adams' arguments can be so much as shaken," the *Southern Review* thought historians dealing in black insinuations were "little worthy of credit, especially when their oblique methods affect the character of a celebrated woman." The *Review* struck the sectional note that would mark the Smith controversy for decades:

"If Pocahontas, alas, had only been born on the barren soil of New England, then would she have been so beautiful as she was brave. As it is, however, both her personal character and her charms are assailed by knights of the New England chivalry of the present day."

The Yankee knights had only begun to fight. Noah Webster's schoolbook gave way to Peter Parley's, which concluded from Smith's life "that persons, at an early age, have very wicked hearts." Moses Coit Tyler and Edward T. Channing, highly respected scholars, found more bluster than veracity in Smith. Charles Dudley Warner observed that the Captain's memory became more vivid as he was further removed by time and space from the events he described.

Edward D. Neill went further. In *Captain John Smith, Adventurer and Romancer,* he pronounced Smith's coat of arms a forgery, found the Pocahontas rescue incredible, and labeled Smith's works "published exaggerations." Neill's *Pocahontas and Her Companions* attacked not only Pocahontas but also her husband, John Rolfe. This, Virginians thought, was a low blow; for it was Rolfe who had perfected the process of curing tobacco, which gave the colony a money crop; it was he who won the hand of the Princess, which gave Virginia peace at a time when the Indians might have driven the colonists into the sea. And what did Neill say of this wedding? He said it was a disgraceful fraud!

Virginians rallied to the defense of their hero, and leading the attack was William Wirt Henry, Patrick Henry's grandson, a lawyer, a state legislator, and president of the American Historical Association. In 1882 he published "The Settlement of Jamestown, with Particular Reference to the Late Attack upon Captain John Smith, Pocahontas, and John Rolfe." With care and ingenuity he evolved explanations for the questionable parts of their stories.

Henry never doubted that the success of the Virginia Colony had depended on the Captain. "The departure of Smith changed the whole aspect of affairs. The Indians at once became hostile, and killed

These engravings from Smith's Generall Historie of Virginia, New-England, and the Summer Isles, *depict the landing of the colonists*

all that came in their way." To the Indian princess Pocahontas he assigned a religious role and mission. She was, in Henry's opinion, "a guardian angel [who] watched over and preserved the infant colony which has developed into a great people, among whom her own descendants have ever been conspicuous for true nobility."

Equally qualified to fight for Smith was Wyndham Robertson, who was raised on a Virginia plantation and chosen to be the state's governor. Northern attacks disturbed him so much that he prepared a detailed study of *Pocahontas alias Matoaka and Her Descendants through Her Marriage with John Rolfe.* Taking the marriage of Pocahontas and Rolfe in 1614 as a focal event, Robertson traced the subsequent family to "its seventh season of fruitage." Among those who turned out to be related to her were the Bollings, Branches, Lewises, Randolphs, and Pages—the very cream of Virginia. Because Pocahontas' descendants were so notable, so was she; this simple a posteriori argument ran through the whole book.

How, asked Robertson, could anyone speak ill of the Princess when the King of England and the Bishop of London had been her devotees? Her natural charm had captivated Mother England. Leaders of society had competed for her favor. She had occupied a special seat when Ben Jonson's Twelfth Night masque was staged at Whitehall; her portrait revealed a truly aristocratic countenance. "With festival, state, and pompe" the Lord Mayor of London had feted her before death cut short her dazzling career. "History, poetry, and art," wrote Robertson, "have vied with one another in investing her name from that day to the present with a halo of surpassing brightness."

Then from across the seas came an unexpected and devastating blow.

It was struck by a Hungarian historian and journalist, Lewis L. Kropf. Born in Budapest and trained as an engineer, he spent most of his life working and writing in London. He combed the British Museum for hitherto unknown material on English-Hungarian relations, and between 1880 and 1913 wrote copiously for Hungarian and English journals of history. He had a predilection for setting others right and for unmasking heroes, and his reputation, as well as his list of publications, grew.

In 1890 Kropf decided to scrutinize Smith's account of his 1601–02 adventures in southeastern Europe. His findings, published in the British *Notes and Queries,* were damning. Not only the places but also the people in Smith's account were pure fictions, said Kropf. At best, his tales should be viewed as "pseudo-historical romance." Very likely John Smith had never got to southeast Europe at all.

British and American scholars, unable to re-examine the obscure Hungarian documents Kropf cited, took him at his word. They concluded that the swashbuckling Englishman was—at least so far as his pre-Virginia story was concerned—a liar. If he was this unreliable about Hungary, how could he be trusted when he wrote of Virginia? His defenders were stunned and silent.

It was sixty years before the answer came. In the 1950's another lady, this time a Hungarian historian, came forth to rescue John Smith, and, so far as his

CONTINUED ON PAGE 110

me of Smith's triumphs and defeats among the Indians, and (at far right) *the Captain's celebrated rescue by Princess Pocahontas.*

33

ISAAC SINGER

SEWING

An erratic genius and his sober-sided partn

built fortunes which their numerous proge

By PET

Edward Clark, a respectable forty-year-old lawyer, found himself, in the summer of 1851, in a disconcerting position. He was (or so it seemed to Clark) newly yoked in partnership with a man of spectacular depravity, a man so lost to shame as to seem that he had never had any to lose. Everything Clark had discovered about his new partner dismayed him; everything in Clark's character and background demanded that he dissolve the partnership. Yet if he did, a glittering fortune would, he feared, go glimmering. For Clark's wife, the choice was simple. "Sell out," she urged him, "and leave the nasty brute." But still Clark hesitated. He might, he argued, somehow conceal from the world the excesses of his abandoned partner; indeed, with good management and a generous admixture of luck he might pluck good from evil and even succeed in presenting the scoundrel in the unlikely guise of mankind's benefactor. And so Clark decided to stick.

Some odd results can be traced back to that decision. Had he chosen otherwise, baseball's Hall of Fame might not stand at Cooperstown; Marcel Proust would have had to shape somewhat differently the character he called the Marquise de Sainte-Euverte; Time Inc. would have had harder sledding in its early days; Palm Beach would not stand as the lush resort it is today; an excellent gallery of French impressionist paintings would not be offered to the public, improbably, on the Mohawk Trail in Williamstown, Massachusetts; and the incumbent president of the National Association of Manufacturers would be some other. But at the time, Clark's decision was only that he should collaborate with Isaac Merritt Singer in the manufacture and sale of the sewing machine that Singer had invented.

In condemning his new partner Clark made no more shocked a judgment than would all of New York society a few years later. Subsequent chroniclers have likewise looked down their noses at Singer; they have either pilloried him with some disgust as a lecher or with labored hilarity have cited his career as a single-handed effort to disprove the Malthusian hypothesis. A more dispassionate verdict is simply that Singer was born in the wrong time and place. He would have fitted nicely into the Rome of the later Caesars; Renaissance Italy would have made him welcome; it is easy

In 1901 the Singer Company sought to boost its sales of 1,000,0 machines a year with this folder, probably designed to publicize

to imagine him roistering through Europe with the Chevalier de Seingalt, Giacomo Casanova; but that he was too rich for the blood of Pecksniffian New York in the pre-Civil War era there can be no doubt.

What uniformly offended Singer's critics was that in the 36 years from 1834 to 1870 he sired 24 children. From a biological point of view there is nothing exceptional about such an achievement, but socially it was unusual in that, of the five different women who bore his two dozen children, Singer was married to only two; moreover, he managed to involve him-

and his WONDERFUL
MACHINE

...ade their product a household necessity and

...ave spent in ways both beneficent and bizarre

...YON

...awards at the Pan-American Exposition. As early as 1861 Singer was doing more than half its business through far-flung foreign agents.

self with the three others simultaneously. These informal liaisons were all in hand by 1851; hence Clark's dismay and disgust.

Clark had other objections to Singer. He was, in the first place, obviously no gentleman. The eighth of a brood of children born to a poverty-stricken German immigrant millwright, he was hot-tempered, arrogant, and habitually profane. In the second place, he was practically illiterate; indeed, Clark suspected he had never had any formal schooling whatever. As if this were not enough, Singer had spent most of his

adult years as an actor, and he had all the actor's egotism. Sinking even lower, if possible, in the social scale, he had been an advance man for a traveling theatrical troupe. How was it conceivable that such a man could have stumbled upon an important mechanical invention?

There was in fact nothing accidental about Singer's accomplishment. He had from boyhood been adept with machinery; his first efforts to earn his own living, shortly after he had run away from home at the age of twelve, had been as apprentice to a machinist in Rochester, New York. But no matter his talent for it, the trade bored him. Moreover, he was hopelessly stage-struck. Illiterate or no, he committed to memory huge chunks of Shakespeare as well as of various fustian scripts advocating temperance. Here was the life: rollicking about the country with complaisant young actresses, bedazzling small-town girls, swaggering about a stage with a mouthful of iambics—while flowers bloom in the garden, why work?

Only when he found himself irremediably at liberty would young Singer reluctantly consider working at his trade. So resolutely did he fight shy of a regular wage that in twenty years he held only three jobs outside the theater. The first was in New York City with Robert Hoe, the well-known manufacturer of printing presses; by that time he was 24 and already married and a father. The second job was four years later, in 1839; he went to work with an older brother, helping to dig the Illinois waterway at Lockport. He found the drudgery so intolerable that he was inspired to develop his first invention, a machine for drilling rock. Fecklessly, he disposed of his patent rights for $2,000, which he promptly squandered by forming his own theatrical company, the Merritt Players. With a repertory that included *Richard III* and *The Stumbling Block, or, Why a Deacon Gave Up His Wine*, he barnstormed throughout the Midwest, at length fetching up, flat broke, in Fredericksburg, Ohio. This was so tiny a settlement that the only job Singer could find was in a sawmill; here he was obliged to toil for two years before he could hit upon another invention —a machine for carving wood-block type. He patented it, and, in easy stages, came to New York.

He had by now compelling reasons to lay hands on some money. Besides his wife, the former Catharine

Isaac Singer spent his happiest years with Isabella Boyer, his second wife and the last of the many women in his life. This faded snapshot, taken about 1870, shows them with little Winnaretta, the second of their six children.

Maria Haley, whom he had long since left with two children to feed, he had taken up with a comely young woman named Mary Ann Sponsler, who, in the course of tagging around the country with him, had borne him six more children, all out of wedlock. He was approaching his fortieth year, and his time for playing *jeunes premiers* was running out. There was the bank account to consider.

Into Singer's life at this juncture, like a plump hen advancing confidently into a den of foxes, came a would-be capitalist of a commonplace sort. This innocent, a man called George Zieber, paid Singer some $3,000 for the Massachusetts rights to the type-carving device and rented space in a Boston machine shop at 19 Harvard Place, not far from the Old South Meeting House. Singer went along to demonstrate the machine to prospective buyers, but, these proving conspicuous by their scarcity, he found time to take notice of his surroundings.

The chief business of the machine shop, owned by Orson Phelps, was supposed to be the manufacture of sewing machines. Owing to some defect in their design, however, more time was spent in repairing the old than in making the new. This was a monotonously familiar complaint against all the early sewing machines, no matter by whom designed or manufactured.

Actually, by 1850 there was nothing new about the idea of a sewing machine. Patents had been granted in England (1790), Austria (1814), the United States (1826), and France (1830) on mechanical devices for sewing. The French machine was reasonably efficient, but its manufacture was summarily halted by the passion of a mob of Parisian tailors who feared the loss of their livelihood. Something of the same sentiment blocked development of a machine constructed by a remarkable American inventor, Walter Hunt, in 1833. Hunt was the sort of man who could contrive anything if he were given a bit of wire and a half hour; to his credit, among dozens of commodities, are the paper collar and the safety pin. But he was a Quaker with an active conscience about the economic morality of his contraptions, and so, after devising an adequate sewing machine, he referred to his daughter the decision as to whether he should go further with it. She entered a veto—on the ground, as she later testified, that "the introduction of such a machine . . . would be injurious to the interests of hand-sewers. I found that the machine would at that time be very unpopular and . . . refused to use it." In consequence, Hunt decided not to seek a patent.

Such compunctions did not trouble other American inventors, of whom the most important was Elias Howe, Jr., who, on September 10, 1846, was granted a patent on a lock-stitch machine with an eye-pointed needle and shuttle. There was only one difficulty attending on Howe's machine, as well as on others patented about the same time: they didn't work efficiently. Ten letters patent were extended to inventors of mechanical sewing devices in 1849-50; the fourth of them was granted to Lerow & Blodgett late in 1849; and theirs was the machine that Singer inspected with mild interest, a little less than a year later, in Orson Phelps's shop.

Singer thought the machine could be made to work. Phelps was skeptical. "If," he retorted, "you can make a really practical sewing machine, you will make more money in a year than you can in fifty with that carving affair."

Singer reflected. Theretofore he had considered that the manufacture of sewing machines was a paltry business; but maybe Phelps knew what he was talking about. If there was money in it, Singer was interested. Inventors are popularly credited with being under only one goad: What, they are imagined to ask themselves, can I invent that will lighten the load of my fellow man? Nothing could have been further from Isaac Singer's lively mind. He himself put his motive with admirable succinctness. "I don't," he said, "care a damn for the invention. The dimes are what I am after."

And so he bethought him of his wide-eyed financier, Zieber, who had already sunk more than $3,000 into Singer's unsalable type-carving device. Would Zieber submit to a further plucking? Singer had nothing to lose by trying.

In fact, Zieber proved woefully reluctant—in his own words he was "loth to advance any thing out of the small amount yet remaining in my possession, to make experiments." He added: "I became very much disheartened."

Not so Singer, all of whose enormous vitality was already responding to what seemed to him a golden challenge. He directed the full force of his considerable charm on Zieber, and, on September 18, 1850, the three men concluded an agreement, drawn up by Zieber. The capitalist was to "furnish the sum of Forty Dollars"; Singer was to "contribute his inventive genius"; Phelps was to provide "his best mechanical skill." The contract was, Zieber later maintained plaintively, "sufficient to secure to each the interest to which he was entitled, had all the other parties been honorably disposed."

And now attend, for Isaac Singer is approaching the moment of his life that will ensure him lasting fame, and the first of the world's important household appliances is about to be born.

The circumstances of the invention itself are obscured by clouds of contention. Zieber later deprecated Singer's role, but his was clearly a prejudiced statement. The canonical account of Singer's triumph, published a quarter century later, bore the inventor's

name as author, but also the unmistakable, ghostly trace of a company publicity man. It is like all such accounts: the humble man of talent works feverishly (eighteen and twenty hours a day), single-mindedly (only one meal a day), for a ridiculously brief time (only eleven days—for, after all, how long would forty dollars last?); at length the parts are assembled on the eleventh night; the assembled machine repeatedly refuses to function, whilst one by one the workmen take their leave, as though from the proverbial sinking ship; the inventor despairs; a chance remark from a bystander leads to the flash of realization of what has been wrong; the tiny adjustment is made, and—eureka!

Whether all this is blarney or not, one stubborn fact stands out: Isaac Singer had developed the first sewing machine that would work.

Nor is it possible to ascribe the invention to the luck of a rascal. Singer's was a brilliant, perceptive, and original design. Andrew B. Jack of the Massachusetts Institute of Technology, whose studies of early sewing-machine history were aided by examination of all the Singer Company's early letter books, has stated that, to be practical, the device must include ten features: (1) lock stitch; (2) eye-pointed needle; (3) shuttle for second thread, vibratory or double-pointed; (4) continuous thread from spools; (5) horizontal table; (6) overhanging arm; (7) contin-

Singer's partner, steady, sensible Edward Clark, managed the merchandising end of the enterprise.

uous feed, synchronous with needle motion; (8) thread or tension controls, giving slack thread as needed; (9) presser foot; and (10) ability to sew in a straight or curving line. Of all these features, only the ninth and tenth were invented by Singer. Elias Howe had originated the first, second, and fourth; other mechanics, notably J. Bachelder and A. B. Wilson, were responsible for the others; but theirs, like all the early machines, were crude and flawed. Only Singer's embraced all ten features.

Singer's design, which has survived substantially intact, was a radical departure from those of all his contemporaries, but it worked; it was, moreover, adaptable to a variety of jobs, whether in the home or the factory. In contrast, Howe's machine could sew only eighteen stitches before the operator was obliged to remove the cloth for a fresh start; and his tension device was imperfect, so that the thread broke repeatedly. "Credit for the invention of the sewing-machine," Jack declares, "must go to Isaac Merritt Singer." It is difficult to overestimate the importance of his accomplishments.

On the heels of his achievement, Singer visibly expanded. His voice, always resonant, now took on a note of authority quite galling to his two associates. When Phelps suggested that, according to their agreement, his name should be linked with Singer's on the patent application, Singer peremptorily shouted him down. When Zieber attempted to mediate and pacify, Singer hectored both men impartially while privately he urged Zieber to buy up Phelps's interest. When Zieber refused, Singer did the job himself, paying Phelps off from money belonging to all three. In short, he behaved like a ruthless man of business whilst his partners behaved like gentle chuckleheads.

Elias Howe now appeared. Howe was uncomfortably aware that his own machine was less practical than Singer's; he was, moreover, in desperate need of money. On the other hand, he had the basic patent, while Singer as yet had none. Manifestly, there was here the basis for a deal if all hands were reasonable. Howe offered Singer and Zieber the American rights to his patent for $2,000. The niceties of patent law were not calculated to appeal to Singer. He reacted in honest and forthright fashion: he would, he declared, boot Howe downstairs if he didn't clear off the premises under his own steam. In part this gesture must have been motivated by the fact that Singer was finding himself, pleasurably and unexpectedly, with money on his hands. His machine, almost from the start, sold well, and the unit profit was generous. The world was becoming his oyster. He and Zieber decided to move their headquarters from Boston to New York.

The move involved, for the romantic inventor, a measure of intrepidity. Somewhere in New York was his wife, whom he had long since deserted (he called her Maria); there, too, was his consort, Mary Ann Sponsler (he called her Mary); and, under two different roofs, there were his children, who now numbered nine. But he had an imperative motive for settling once again in New York. The fact was, love had come again to Singer, in the shape of Mary Eastwood Walters (he called her Mary), 28 years old and presently the mother of his tenth child. He had not been in New York very long before love came to him again—for he was nothing if not receptive to the little naked god—in the shape of Mary McGonigal (how convenient; he could call her Mary, too), 22 years old and presently the mother of his eleventh child.

All this love cost the inventor money. Indeed, by early in 1851, his expenses were so considerable that the partnership of Singer and Zieber was obliged to open its arms to a third man, Barzillan Ransom, an elderly gentleman from Brooklyn who manufactured cloth bags for salt and was sufficiently impressed by Singer's machine to tender promissory notes worth up to $10,000 in return for a one-third share in the business. But Ransom did not last long. To Singer he was merely another pigeon. Ransom, on the other hand, found Singer an extraordinary specimen, of a kind he had never before had an opportunity to inspect at close range. In March he termed Singer "singular"; by April he had concluded Singer was a "dictator . . . insufferable and unless he alters his hand promptly we must separate." By May he had withdrawn—without having paid his notes.

Here was a blow, but there was worse to come. Elias Howe, angered by the success of various sewing-machine manufacturers and thoroughly embittered by a personal tragedy that he blamed on his earlier poverty, had turned vengefully litigious. He brandished suits, one after another, for patent infringement. From Singer he demanded $25,000. Payment of such a sum was of course out of the question, even presuming Singer for a moment believed he had infringed. He was certain he had not; but he needed a lawyer to prove his case, and he had no money even for a lawyer. He appealed to Ambrose Jordan, the attorney who had accompanied him to Washington when he applied for a patent. Would Jordan, Singer inquired, handle the case—and any subsequent litigation—for a share in the business? Jordan refused, for he found Singer personally distasteful. Instead, he referred him to his junior partner and son-in-law, Edward Clark. A former Sunday school teacher, a graduate of Williams at a time when that college's undergraduate body consisted almost wholly of pros-

CONTINUED ON PAGE 103

Comic trade cards (above) were handed out in the 1890's to buyers, would-be buyers, and agents for Singer's newfangled machine. The travel cards (below) were widely distributed at country fairs and testify to the ubiquity of the founder's sales force, which canvassed from the frozen tundra of Archangel to the coral reefs of the Caroline Islands.

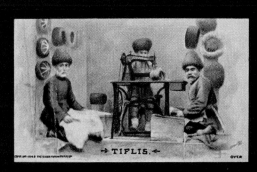

Harper's Weekly, AUGUST, 18(

It took a decade of effort, heart-breaking disappointments, and the largest ship afloat before Cyrus Field could lay a successful cable across the Atlantic

By ARTHUR C. CLARKE

The American warship Niagara (center) *and two escorts (U.S.S.* Susquehanna, *at left, and H.M.S.* Leopard) *prepare to leave Valentia Bay in May, 1857, in a Robert Dudley painting. The whale boats are bringing in the cable's shore end.*

Cyrus West Field was one of the greatest Americans of the nineteenth century, but today there can be few of his countrymen who remember him. He opened up no frontiers, killed no Indians, founded no industrial empires, won no battles; the work he did has been buried deep in the Atlantic ooze for almost one hundred years. Yet he helped to change history, and now that his dream of a telegraph to Europe has been surpassed by a still more wonderful achievement, the transatlantic telephone cable, it is only right that we should pay tribute to the almost superhuman courage which enabled him to triumph over repeated disasters.

His face is looking at me now, across the century that lies between us. It is not at all the face of the international financier or the company promoter, though Field was both these things. The thin, sensitive nose, the regular features, the deep-set, brooding eyes—these add up to a poet or musician, not to the stereotyped sad success, indistinguishable from all his ulcer-ridden colleagues we see today in the business section of *Time* magazine. "Visionary and chivalrous" were the words applied to Field many years later, and no one without vision would have set off on the long and arduous quest that dominated his life for almost twelve years.

[A New Englander by birth, Field had already made a fortune in the wholesale paper business by the time he was 33, but the effort had taken a heavy toll on his health, and he had been ordered by his doctors to relax. He took a trip to Europe with his wife, then toured South America with the famous landscape painter Frederick E. Church. To all intents and purposes Field, a millionaire by today's standards and still a young man, had retired for good.]

He might have remained in retirement for the rest of his days if chance had not brought him into contact with F. N. Gisborne, an English engineer engaged in building a telegraph line across Newfoundland. When the Newfoundland company went bankrupt in 1853 before more than forty miles of line had been erected, Gisborne, who had been left holding the company's debts, went to New York the next year in an attempt to raise more money for the scheme. By good fortune he met Cyrus Field, who was then relaxing after his South American trip and was not at all keen on becoming involved in any further business undertakings. He listened politely to Gisborne but did not commit himself to any promise of help. Only the uncompleted line across Newfoundland was discussed, but when the meeting was over and he was alone in his library, Field started to play with the globe and suddenly realized that the Newfoundland telegraph

was merely one link in a far more important project. Why wait for steamers to bring news from Europe? Let the telegraph do the whole job.

From that moment, Field became obsessed with the Atlantic telegraph. True, he was not the first man to conceive of a submarine cable linking Europe and America. In 1843 Samuel F. B. Morse, after successful experiments with an underwater telegraph cable in New York Harbor, had predicted that "telegraphic communication . . . may with certainty be established across the Atlantic Ocean. Startling as this may now seem, I am confident the time will come when the project will be realized." But Cyrus Field was the first to do anything practical. The next morning he wrote letters to Morse and to Lieutenant Matthew Fontaine Maury, founder of the modern science of oceanography.

By one of those coincidences that are inevitable when many people are thinking along the same lines, Maury received Field's letter at a moment when he had written to the secretary of the navy on the same subject. He had forwarded a report of a recent survey of the North Atlantic, carried out by Lieutenant Berryman, disclosing the existence of a plateau between Newfoundland and Ireland. Maury had commented, in a letter to the secretary of the navy on February 22, 1854, that this plateau "seems to have been placed there especially for the purpose of holding the wires of a Submarine Telegraph, and of keeping them out of harm's way."

Field could hardly have hoped for better news, and a few days later Morse called to see him with equally encouraging advice. With the world's greatest names in oceanography and telegraphy to back him up, Field now had only to convince the financiers.

[Field turned first to his next-door neighbor in New York, the influential millionaire Peter Cooper, and with his backing and that of several other capitalists he went to Newfoundland in 1854, paid the debts of Gisborne's company, and obtained exclusive rights for all cables touching Newfoundland and Labrador for the next fifty years. With these tangible assets, he managed to raise $1,250,000 in New York and organized the New York, Newfoundland and London Telegraph Company, which opened a New York-to-Newfoundland line in 1856, as a first stage for a transatlantic cable.

Meanwhile, Field had helped promote new British-American surveys of the North Atlantic which showed that, although the so-called "Telegraph Plateau" was

From *Voice Across the Sea* by Arthur Charles Clarke. Copyright © 1958 by Arthur Charles Clarke. Published by Harper & Brothers.

not quite as flat as originally supposed, its slopes were not prohibitively severe. What was more, its greatest distance from the surface was less than 15,000 feet—and submarine cables had already been laid as deep as this.

Unable to obtain all the backing he needed on this side of the Atlantic, in 1856 Field went to England. There Professor Morse constructed a replica of the proposed Atlantic cable by connecting ten circuits each 200 miles long (using the London-Birmingham line) and succeeded in passing up to 200 signals a minute through it. On the strength of Morse's successful results, Field obtained a British treasury subsidy of £14,000 a year—4 per cent of the £350,000 capital that the project was expected to cost—for the consideration that the prospective telegraph company would

Harper's Weekly, AUGUST, 1865

Pres.t JOHNSON reading the morning's news from EUROPE.

give British government messages priority over everything but those of the American government. In addition, the British Navy pledged facilities for surveying the route and laying the cable.]

The cast of characters for the forthcoming production was now assembled. The most important was a brilliant young telegraph engineer named Charles Tilson Bright, who at the incredible age of 24 now became chief engineer for one of the most ambitious projects of the century.

Charles Bright was another of those phenomenal Victorians who sometimes make one wonder if the human race has since deteriorated. When only nineteen he had laid a complete system of telegraph wires under the streets of Manchester in a single night without causing any disturbance to traffic. A year later he had taken out 24 patents for basic inventions, some of which—such as the porcelain insulator for overhead wires—are still in use.

A man of action as well as a brilliant engineer,

Bright became a member of Parliament at 33 and died at the early age of 55, burned out by his exertions. His monument is a network of telegraph cables stretching more than halfway round the globe and linking together all the countries of the world.

Bright had become interested in the Atlantic telegraph even earlier than Field. Between 1853 and 1855 he had conducted experiments to study the propagation of signals through two thousand miles of line, using for this purpose the ten circuits of 200 miles each between London and Manchester, connected in series. In the summer of 1855 he had carried out a survey of the Irish coast and had decided that Valentia Bay, near the southwest tip of Ireland, was the best place to land a transatlantic cable. This decision has been endorsed by every company which has taken a cable to Ireland for the last hundred years.

A much less fortunate appointment was that of Dr. Edward Orange Wildman Whitehouse as the company's electrician. Dr. Whitehouse was a Brighton surgeon who had interested himself in telegraphy and had acquired a considerable knowledge of the subject by practical experimenting. He was a man of strong personality and fixed ideas, and although his enthusiasm did much to get the company started in its early days, his refusal to recognize his limitations was later to bring disaster.

The first meeting of the Atlantic Telegraph Company took place at Liverpool on November 12, 1856, and Field, Bright, and John Watkins Brett, a retired antique dealer who with his brother Jacob had laid a cable across the English Channel in 1850, outlined the commercial prospects of the enterprise with such effect that the entire £350,000 was subscribed in a few days. Field took up £75,000 of this, not for his own benefit but on behalf—as he fondly imagined—of his fellow Americans. When he got back to his own country, however, he had the utmost difficulty in unloading even £27,000 of this amount and was left holding the remainder himself.

Most of the capital was taken up by British business houses, though among the private subscribers it is interesting to note the names of Lady Byron and William Makepeace Thackeray. These literary figures were obviously keener on progress than their contemporary Thoreau, who had written in *Walden* two years before:

We are in great haste to construct a magnetic telegraph from Maine to Texas; but Maine and Texas, it may be, have nothing important to communicate. We are eager to tunnel under the Atlantic and bring the Old World some weeks nearer to the New; but perchance the first news that will leak through into the broad, flapping American ear will be that Princess Adelaide has the whooping-cough. . . .

[Field expected the same co-operation from his own government as he had received in Britain, but in Washington he ran into congressional opposition, based partly on financial grounds (several congressmen objected to the $70,000 a year the government would have to pay for telegraph service), and partly on fear of political entanglements—Senator James C. Jones of Tennessee remarking that "he did not want anything to do with England or Englishmen." But on March 3, 1857, by a single vote, a bill was passed granting the subsidy which would guarantee a steady income for the cable company and providing for ships to help in the cable-laying.]

A thankful but somewhat exhausted Cyrus Field hurried back to England to see how his British colleagues were faring. They were making fine progress, spinning out cable at a rate that has seldom been matched since, and ought not to have been attempted then. Largely because Field had promised his backers that the telegraph would start working in 1857, specifications had been sent out to the manufacturers even before the board of management had been set up, and the production of the cable in the short time of six months was a remarkable performance. It involved drawing and spinning 335,000 miles of iron and copper wire and covering that with 300,000 miles of tarred hemp to form a cable 2,500 miles long. (The actual distance from Ireland to Newfoundland is about 500 miles less than this, but the extra length was needed for slack in paying out and to allow for possible losses.)

The company's engineers were not helped by streams of advice and criticism from outside experts, such as the astronomer royal, Sir George Airy, who stated dogmatically that "it was a mathematical impossibility to submerge the cable in safety at so great a depth, and if it were possible, no signals could be transmitted through so great a length. . . ." When distinguished scientists made such fools of themselves, it is easy to excuse the numerous inventors who wrote to Bright with proposals based on the ancient fallacy that heavy objects did not sink to the sea bed, but eventually came to rest at a level where their density was matched by that of the surrounding water. There is, of course, no truth in this idea, for water is so nearly incompressible that even at the greatest depths encountered in the ocean its density is only very slightly greater than at sea level.

Some of the hopeful inventors wished to suspend the cable in mid-ocean by underwater parachutes or balloons; others even more optimistically wanted to connect it to a string of floating call boxes across the Atlantic, so that ships could keep in touch with land as they crossed from continent to continent. Whether they were crazy or not, Charles Bright replied politely to all these proposals, few of which were inhibited by the slightest practical knowledge of the oceanographic and telegraphic facts of life.

The Atlantic Telegraph Company, in any event, had little need for outside help. On its own board of directors was a scientific genius (and for once the word is not misapplied) who was later to do more than any man to save the lost cause of submarine telegraphy and to retrieve the company's fortunes.

William Thomson, Lord Kelvin, was not the greatest scientist of the nineteenth century; on any reasonable list, he must come below Darwin and Maxwell. But it is probable that he was the most famous man of science of his age, the one whom the general public

Harper's Weekly, AUGUST, 1865

Queen VICTORIA reading the news from AMERICA.

chiefly identified with the astonishing inventions and technical advances of the era.

In this, public opinion was correct, for Thomson was a unique bridge between the laboratory and the world of industry. He was an "applied scientist" par excellence, using his wonderful insight to solve urgent practical problems. Yet he was very much more than this, being also one of the greatest of mathematical physicists. The range of his interests and activities was enormous; the multiplication of knowledge that has taken place since his time makes it impossible that we will see his like again. It would not be unfair to say that if one took half the talents of Einstein and half the talents of Edison, and succeeded in fusing such incompatible gifts into a single person, the result would be rather like William Thomson.

Thomson became involved in the telegraph story as a result of his investigations into what are known as transient electric currents. What happens, he asked himself in 1853, when a battery is connected up to a circuit, in the minute interval of time before the current settles down to its steady value? At one moment nothing is happening; a fraction of a second later, a current of some definite amount is flowing. The problem was to discover what took place during the transition period, which is seldom as much as a hundredth of a second in duration, and is usually very much shorter.

Nothing could have seemed of less practical importance. Yet these studies led directly to the understanding of all electrical communication, and, some thirty years later, to the discovery of radio waves.

Thomson began to investigate the behavior of telegraph cables. It is possible to understand his main results, and to appreciate their importance, without any knowledge of the mathematics he used to obtain them. Putting it briefly, the problem involved was this: How long does it take for a signal to reach the far end of a telegraph cable?

It is a common error to imagine that electricity travels along a wire at the speed of light—186,000 miles a second. This is never true, although in some circumstances this velocity can be approached. In most cases, the speed of a current is very much less than that of light—sometimes, indeed, only a tenth or a hundredth of its value.

This slowing-down is due to the electrical capacity of the line. A telegraph cable behaves very much like a hose pipe; it takes a certain amount of electricity to "fill it up" before there is any appreciable result at the other end.

Fortunately for the progress of the telegraphic art, this effect was of no practical importance in the early days of land lines. Their capacity was so low that messages passed through them without any appreciable delay, and it was not until the first submarine cables were laid across the English Channel and the North Sea that signal-retardation became a source of trouble. Its prime cause is the presence of the conducting sea water which surrounds a cable and thus greatly increases its capacity. Because of this effect, a cable may need twenty times as much electricity to charge it up when it is submerged as it would require if suspended in air.

Thomson's analysis led him to his famous "law of squares," which states that the speed with which messages can be sent through a given cable decreases with the square of its length. In other words, if one multiplies the length of a cable ten times, the rate of signaling will be reduced a hundredfold. This law is obviously of fundamental importance in long-distance submarine telegraphy; the only way of circumventing it is to increase the size of the conducting core.

This was not appreciated by all telegraph engineers, and was even denied by some—including, unfortunately, Dr. Whitehouse. He had carried out experiments purporting to refute the law of squares; these had also led him to conclude (and the same views had been expressed by Faraday and Morse) that a small conducting wire might be better than a large one, which was the exact reverse of the truth. When such confusion prevailed among the "experts," it is hardly surprising that the first Atlantic cable was badly designed. It had about as much chance of success as a bridge built by engineers who did not understand the laws governing the strength of materials.

Thomson was only one of the company's directors, and had no authority—beyond his scientific prestige—over the men who were in charge of its technical affairs. Because of their determination to lay the cable during the summer of 1857, the promoters of the scheme had left no time for the experiments and tests which were essential for its success. The dynamic energy of Cyrus Field was partly responsible for this, and when Thomson arrived on the scene, he discovered that the specifications for the cable had already been sent out to the manufacturers and that it was now too late to alter them. What was more, when he had an opportunity of testing the completed article, he was shocked to discover that the quality of the copper varied so much that some sections conducted twice as well as others. There was nothing that could be done, except to insist that future lengths be made of the purest possible copper and to hope that the existing cable would be good enough for the job.

The conductor itself consisted of seven strands of copper wire twisted together and insulated by three separate layers of gutta-percha. If there was a hole or imperfection in one layer, the other two would still provide adequate protection. Only in the extremely improbable event of three flaws occurring in exactly the same place would there be danger of an electrical failure.

The insulated core was then covered with a layer of hemp, which in turn was armored with eighteen strands of twisted iron wire. The resulting cable was

TEXT CONTINUED ON PAGE 85

A PORTFOLIO OF ILLUSTRATIONS BEGINS ON THE OPPOSITE PAGE

In 1866 a remarkable book appeared, The Atlantic Telegraph, *by William Howard Russell, one of the most eminent newspaper correspondents of his day. He had covered both the Crimean War and the American Civil War for the London* Times, *and he was the only reporter on board the* Great Eastern *during the cable-laying. Russell's book is illustrated with paintings by the artist Robert Dudley, who was also on board. On the following pages are reproduced a selection of the illustrations Dudley prepared for Russell's narrative.*

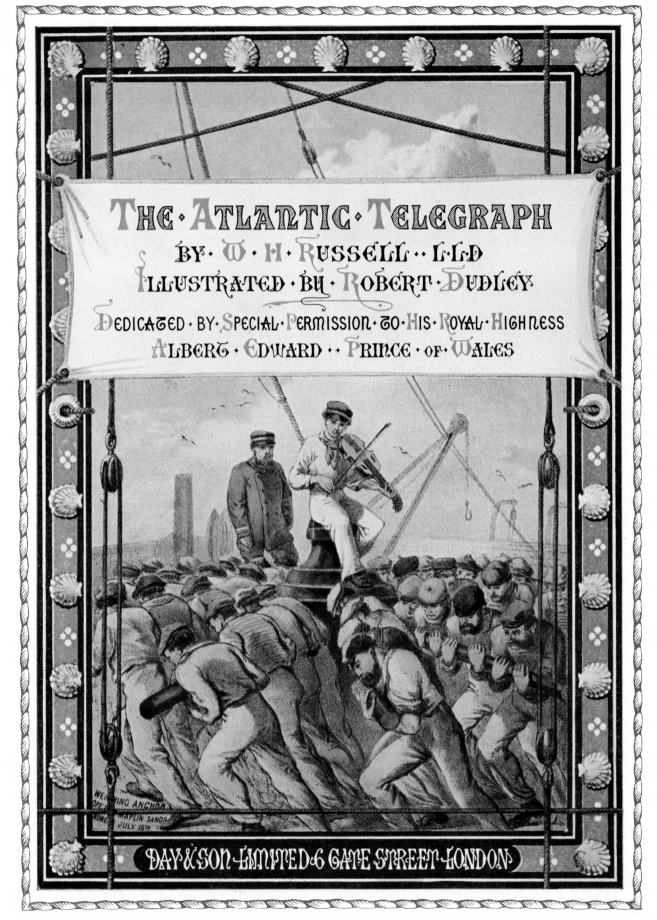

THE · ATLANTIC · TELEGRAPH

BY · W · H · RUSSELL · LLD

ILLUSTRATED · BY · ROBERT · DUDLEY

DEDICATED · BY · SPECIAL · PERMISSION · TO · HIS · ROYAL · HIGHNESS

ALBERT · EDWARD · · PRINCE · OF · WALES

WEIGHING ANCHOR
OFF MAPLIN SANDS
JULY 15TH

DAY & SON · LIMITED · 6 GATE STREET · LONDON

Finished cable was ferried out to the Great Eastern *in the Medway River by ancient men-of-war turned into barges.*

The mammoth Great Eastern *dwarfs her escort ships as they begin their westward voyage from Ireland, July 23, 1865.*

Workmen guard against fouling as the cable passes out from one of the three tanks in the hold of the Great Eastern.

Success in laying the cable depended on the operation of this paying-out machinery on the deck of the Great Eastern.

A tense moment of the 1858 cable-laying, which was also covered in Russell's book, came when the Agamemnon met "a very large whal

. . and great was the relief of all when the ponderous living mass was seen slowly to pass astern, just grazing the cable. . . ."

Fearful of sabotage, technicians examine a faulty section of the cable recovered from the floor of the Atlantic.

Having failed to raise the broken end of the cable, the Great Eastern *lowers a buoy to mark the spot for a new try.*

In the bows of the Great Eastern *on August 2, 1865, men prepare to grapple, without success, for the lost cable.*

The telegraph house at Heart's Content, Newfoundland, served as the western terminus of the transatlantic cable.

A retrospect of the
Sacco-Vanzetti trial
TRAGEDY IN DEDHAM

By FRANCIS RUSSELL

Bartolomeo Vanzetti (left) and Nicola Sacco, by Ben Shahn.

On the afternoon of April 15, 1920, in South Braintree, Massachusetts, two gunmen killed a paymaster and his guard, seized the $16,000 payroll, and escaped. Nicola Sacco and Bartolomeo Vanzetti were picked up by police and identified by several witnesses as the holdup men. In 1921, at the conclusion of a trial in Dedham, the two men were found guilty of murder. The leisurely legal processes of exception and appeal, however, went on for six years; in that period many people came to feel that the trial had been unfair and that Sacco and Vanzetti had been convicted not because they were murderers, but because they were anarchists. In June, 1927, the late Governor Alvan T. Fuller appointed a committee of review composed of Judge Robert Grant, President Samuel W. Stratton of the Massachusetts Institute of Technology, and A. Lawrence Lowell, president of Harvard. The Lowell Committee concluded that the trial had been fair and made no recommendation for clemency. Sacco and Vanzetti were executed in the early morning hours of August 23, 1927, in the Charlestown State Prison.

The case of Sacco and Vanzetti, which began as the prosecution for a commonplace if brutal murder, developed gradually into one of the world's great trials. In the end it was much more than a trial. It became one of those events that divide a society. Although the issues that it raised have been overlaid by war and political events, they never wholly die. Even today middle-aged men and women hearing by some chance the names Sacco and Vanzetti still find themselves stirred by the passion and violence of their younger days. Sacco and Vanzetti have become a symbol, and like all symbols the meaning varies with those who adopt it.

I myself do not have any memory of the 1921 trial, I then being in the fifth grade of the Boston public schools, but I do remember from my seventeenth year the agitation and excitement of those summer weeks in 1927 preceding the two men's execution. The day they were to die I took the elevated in to Boston and spent the better part of the afternoon walking over Beacon Hill and across the Common in the August sunshine. In spite of the tranquillity of the weather the atmosphere was tense. Police were everywhere, hard-faced and angry, some of them carrying rifles— a thing I had never seen before. Pickets with placards marched up and down before the Bulfinch façade of the State House. Periodically the police carted groups of them away in a patrol wagon to the Joy Street Station. Almost at once their places were filled by others. Buses kept arriving from New York hung with signs announcing that "Sacco and Vanzetti Must Not Die!" and trailing red paper streamers. As the buses pulled into Park Street those inside began to sing "The Red Flag." They looked like foreigners, most of them. I did not like their looks. Crossing Boston Common on that hot afternoon I sensed in myself the hostility of the bourgeois world toward these two men. In spite of any pickets and red-streamered buses from New York, I knew that they were going to die that night. As I walked under the faintly scented lindens on the Tremont Street side of the Frog Pond, I felt a sense of oneness with the community that was asserting itself. I was glad Sacco and Vanzetti were going to die.

It never occurred to me that the two men might be innocent. In the shabby-genteel little private school I went to in Roxbury none of the masters would have dreamed of such a thing. We took our opinions from them and from our parents. The father of one of my classmates was court reporter of Massachusetts. He had written a much approved pamphlet, *Sacco and Vanzetti in the Scales of Justice,* in which he had demonstrated the quasi-divine status of Massachusetts justice, a status which made even the appointment of the Lowell Committee to investigate the case a reflection on the Commonwealth's judicial system. According to the reporter that system, so sanctified by the past, could not err. Such a conservative position was common enough in Massachusetts then. Nor did it change. Thirty years later the reporter still listed his pamphlet in the American *Who's Who* as his single literary accomplishment.

By and large one's view of the case depended on one's status in the community. If one were middle-class and Republican and read the *Herald* mornings and the *Transcript* nights, one thought Sacco and Vanzetti were guilty. Any latent doubts subsided after President Lowell of Harvard issued his report. But if one were a university liberal one tended to think the trial unfair, and if one read the *Nation* or *New Republic* one was sure they were innocent.

My father was a lawyer and a Republican. He believed the two men guilty, not from any particular study of the trial itself but because of his acquaintance with Captain Van Amburgh, a ballistics expert who testified at the trial. Captain Van Amburgh through laboratory examinations was certain that one of the recovered murder bullets had been fired from Sacco's gun. This convinced my father, although—as it came out later—it never convinced Captain Proctor of the State Police.

My Aunt Amy, who was a social worker and lived in the Elizabeth Peabody House, was equally convinced of the two men's innocence. This again was not from studying the evidence—I don't think Aunt Amy did anything more than glance at Professor Frankfurter's book—but that was the way one had to feel if one were a social worker. Nobody could have continued to stay at the Elizabeth Peabody House who felt otherwise—not that such a person would ever have been there in the first place. One of the proud moments of Aunt Amy's life was when she was arrested for picketing the State House and taken away in the patrol wagon. I think she was almost disappointed that the policeman who arrested her was so courteous about it.

I can remember Sundays after dinner when my father and Aunt Amy would get to wrangling about the case, not arguing from logic but merely making mutually contradictory statements. One afternoon Aunt Amy struck the table and called my father a liar. Neither one of them was the least bit interested in the other's point of view. After the publication of the Lowell Report my father maintained that Frankfurter should have resigned from the Harvard Law School. Aunt Amy's high opinion of the Lowells was never quite the same again.

I don't know when my views about Sacco and Vanzetti changed. It must have been some time in the thirties, when I happened to read their letters. Those letters just weren't compatible with the sordid and mercenary Braintree murders. As to the question of who were the murderers if Sacco and Vanzetti were not, I found that answered later in a book by one of their counsel, Herbert B. Ehrmann's *The Untried Case,* which seemed to prove conclusively enough that the men who did the killing were from the Morelli Gang of Providence. If one accepted that explanation, reinforced by more factual evidence as time went on, everything fitted together, even to the number of men involved. For all witnesses agreed that there were five men in the murder car, although the prosecution never attempted to account for more than two. One of the Morellis looked enough like Sacco to have been his brother.

Dedham, where the trial took place, is one of those quiet backwaters that span the decades without ever causing much comment until suddenly, and much to the regret of the townspeople, it is made known by the event. For the most part it is a mill town stretched along the loops of the Charles River. But the older section near the High—not Main—Street is a well-preserved relic of the Colonial past. This High Street, overarched by elms, has its spacious frame houses of the mid-eighteenth century and its later and more grandiloquent mansions of the century's end. It has two graceful white meetinghouses and a Victorian granite Episcopal church with an English-type churchyard where deans and a bishop lie buried. The Courthouse on the High Street, built in 1827, is a stone building with massive Greek-revival columns. Its Roman-style dome, soberly proportioned to the columns, is the most characteristic object in Dedham. From the flat country beyond the river it looms above the elms, flanked by the meetinghouse spires, a symbol of authority.

I have seen its silhouette from across the marshes in all seasons of the year. That stretch of bogland beyond U.S. 1, those miles of buttonbush and hardhack and speckled alder, converges on the horizon line of the Courthouse dome. Almost always when I see the great dome so secure above the peaceful community I find myself thinking back to the Sacco-Vanzetti trial. Its ghost still seems to linger over the Courthouse and the High Street, a tangible presence, whatever one's feelings may be about it.

I felt that presence even more keenly in 1953, 32 years after the trial, when I was called on to serve for a month as a juror in that domed Courthouse, in the same aloof paneled room where Sacco and Vanzetti were tried and found guilty and, after all the exceptions and delays, were sentenced to death six years later.

Scarcely a day of that month passed but there was some reference to the Sacco-Vanzetti trial. In Dedham, at least, there were no longer any feelings of partisanship about it. Yet everyone sensed somehow that for the town it had been the climactic event.

The old sheriff in his blue serge cutaway with the large brass buttons had served there for forty years. He had been deputy sheriff in the First World War, and was made sheriff the year before the Sacco-Vanzetti trial. Sometimes during the long lunch hour one of us would ask about the trial and he would reminisce. All his loyalty and most of his life were bound up with the Dedham court. The law revealed there was majestically certain. I don't think he ever entertained the idea it might err, nor do I think his mind ever questioned the Sacco-Vanzetti decision. A due process of law was final. To think otherwise would be to challenge the very things that had become part of him—his brass buttons, his white wand of office with the blue state seal on it. His office did not however keep him from having personal feelings apart from the law. He had come to like Sacco and Vanzetti. "They were good boys," he told us. "I knew Nick best, but they were both good boys. Never any trouble in jail. Now those Millens—you remember them? They were really bad eggs. You had to keep your eye on them every minute."

Sometimes at the end of the afternoon session he would take a few of us through the jail two streets away, and after showing us the reception hall and the dining room and the laundry would always point out the cells of Sacco and Vanzetti. "I was in the court," he told us one afternoon as we stood in front of the barred door, "that day when Judge Thayer sentenced them. Vanzetti made his speech first, that long speech—maybe you heard about it. And all the time he was talking Judge Thayer just sat there with his chin in his hand looking down at his desk. Never moved. But when Vanzetti finished, then he let him have it."

Just outside the courtroom in the tessellated corridor we would pass the prisoners' cage, used in all Massachusetts murder trials. In this cage the defendants Sacco and Vanzetti sat, as have all other Norfolk County defendants. The cage has often been mentioned in the literature of the case, as if the two men had been exhibited in court like monkeys in a zoo. But in spite of its name the cage is no cage at all. It is a topless enclosure of woven metal lattice about three feet high in front rising to five feet in the back. Inside is a bench; at either end are latched doors. Except for its symbolism there is nothing very formidable about it.

I was on a civil jury. Most of our cases concerned car accidents and personal injuries. One of our last cases, a minor one involving a woman who had cut her leg in the door of a car, made the courtroom buzz as it began. The lawyer for the plaintiff seemed to be the cause of it, for as soon as he appeared there was a wave of whispering. Even the clerk came over to the rail and muttered something quickly to our foreman. The lawyer was a portly man in his sixties or seventies, with a manner so assured that it was almost contemptuous. He was baldish, his face florid, with the flesh sagging under the cheeks. Behind his rimless spectacles his pale-blue eyes watered. He was dressed with the conservatism of a Boston banker, a hard-woven worsted suit cut in characteristic pear-shaped style. His shoes were of Scotch grain leather, he had a handkerchief tucked in his sleeve, and there were several club seals on his gold watch chain. When he spoke his voice was upper-class Bostonian, that elastic prolongation of the vowel sounds that has come to be known as the Harvard accent. As soon as he opened his argument he lapsed into Victorian rhetoric.

The clerk's remark was passed along the jury box; the man next to me nudged my elbow. "That's Katzmann," he said, "the fellow that got Sacco and Vanzetti."

In his pear-shaped suit he seemed the culmination of the ghosts of the month. There he was again, in Judge Webster Thayer's old courtroom, at the scene of his triumph of a generation before. As I watched him facing us, spinning polysyllabic phrases out of

Vanzetti and Sacco, with their guards, during their trial.

nothing, I tried to form an impression of him divorced altogether from the Sacco-Vanzetti case. If I had seen him only at that moment, I should have thought him empty and pompous, his smugness derived from the fact that he was a Mayflower descendant (as in spite of his name I believe he was). But I should also have admitted his basic honesty. He died the following year.

Some months later I talked with a judge who had known Katzmann. When I told him about Dedham he asked me my opinion of the man. I said he was verbose, third rate, not wholly grammatical. He laughed. "That describes most of us lawyers," he said. "As for Katzmann, he was average—an average district attorney, a little tricky like most of them, but no worse than most out to get a conviction. He thought Sacco and Vanzetti were guilty. I'm sure he never changed his mind."

"What did you think of the trial?" I asked him.

"I don't think the trial was fair. Whether they were guilty or not, I don't think it was fair. Judge Thayer was prejudiced—although like Katzmann, I grant you, he thought they were guilty, guilty of murder and not of just being Reds."

It does not seem to me today that any reasonable-minded person reading over the literature of the Sacco-Vanzetti case could come to any other conclusion than that the two men were innocent. There are aspects of the case that are still inexplicable—but these men were not the stuff of criminals, either in their natures or their habits or even their practical experience. "The dry bones still rattle," Heywood Broun wrote nine years after their execution. They no longer rattle. The case has become part of history. And since then we have become more used to innocent people being condemned. A new generation is scarcely aware of them; the cause they thought they died for is no cause. One finds Vanzetti's noble last address to the court in several anthologies: "If it had not been for this thing, I might have lived out my life talking at street corners to scorning men. I might have died, unmarked, unknown, a failure. Now we are not a failure. This is our career and our triumph." But the words were not prophetic after all.

A third of a century has passed since the trial. Judge Thayer, Katzmann, President Lowell, and most of the jurors and witnesses are dead. What remains out of this shadowed past? Two men were executed for a crime they did not commit. Beyond all partisanship, how could it have been avoided?

The two sides became irreconcilable. One side felt, as did the court reporter in his pamphlet, that anything less than the execution of Sacco and Vanzetti would undermine the Massachusetts judiciary. The

The paintings accompanying this article are part of a series of *gouaches* on the Sacco-Vanzetti case which in 1932 brought to prominence a painter named Ben Shahn, who has since become one of America's most distinguished artists. Shahn's recollections of the trial suggest the depths of passion it aroused among socially-conscious intellectuals both here and in Europe. "I hate injustice," the artist said. "Ever since I could remember I'd wished I'd been lucky enough to be alive at that great time—when something big was going on, like the Crucifixion. And suddenly I realized I was. Here I was living through another crucifixion. Here was something to paint!"

Below: The Lowell Committee. Above: Judge Thayer.

other side demanded that the whole proceedings of Judge Thayer's court be repudiated. There should have been some middle way out, some face-saving formula that would at least have pacified if not contented the reporter and his kind and yet given the men their lives. Whatever the defense's private opinion of Judge Thayer, it would have been better to have said less about him and concentrated on the subsequently discovered evidence. That this evidence, chiefly concerning the Morelli gang, changed nothing was pre-eminently the responsibility of President Lowell. Working as he did in private with his committee, unhampered by strict rules of legal evidence, he had the opportunity to examine all the facts. A word from him, an indirect indication, and Governor Fuller would have stayed the death sentence and ordered a new trial. The Lowell Report is incomprehensible—unless it was that Lowell, the trained and objective historian, took the point of view of a minor court reporter.

Governor Fuller, of course, took his cue from the report. If he, the parvenu, had not been so in awe of Lowell and the Back Bay ascendancy he represented, perhaps he would have acted otherwise. His contact with Sacco and Vanzetti is said to have been friendly.

Once or twice a year going into the State Street Trust building I used to see Fuller. The doorman would see him first and swing the door open with a ringing "Good morning, Governor." I slipped through in the eddy. The old politician billowed ahead of me under full sail. Self-esteem carried him along like a favoring wind. His was the pride of manner that has reached its goal. An Alger story of the new century. From a Malden bicycle shop to the head of the Packard agency for New England when Packard was the Rolls Royce of America. A mansion on the water side of Beacon Street hung with Gainsboroughs and Romneys and Raeburns. That was the first stage. Then the governorship. And when Packard slipped in the depression, the ex-Governor sensed the moment of ebb and shifted to Cadillac.

In these last years of his life, I suppose Sacco and Vanzetti, those men whose hands he shook so long ago in the death cells, had become blurred impressions, half-forgotten, overlaid by eighteenth-century paintings and the tail-fins of Cadillacs. "Our reputation is your protection," said the Governor's used-car "ad." Yet I never saw him swinging into the State Street Trust but I thought of his role in the trial.

Public opinion in Massachusetts—however that nebulous entity can be defined—was against Sacco and Vanzetti. To the community they were two murderers who had been given a fair trial and every opportunity for appeal afterward. The whole thing had gone on for much too long. Radicals and anarchists and Communists were trying to use the case as a lever to pry apart the foundations of law and order. But Massachusetts was not going to be dictated to by such people. There might be demonstrations in front of American embassies throughout the world, there might be more bombs planted in the houses of those concerned —as had already happened to Judge Thayer and one of the jurors. Nothing like that was going to change the course of justice. Conservative opinion more and more adopted the point of view that Sacco and Vanzetti had become a challenge to society that could be answered only by their deaths. This view, though it prevailed judicially, never did have a literate apologia.

Literary talent was the forte of the other side. That side consisted of the literary left, radicals, liberals, Communists, woolly well-meaning progressives like my Aunt Amy, plus a large scattering of people who could not be labeled politically but whose sense of justice had been outraged. Some of these latter were starched conservatives. The crystallized view of the opposition was that Sacco and Vanzetti were the victims of a malignant conspiracy. Neither judge nor district attorney had really believed them guilty of murder. The trial was a put-up job to get rid of two troublesome agitators.

For the Communists—to whom this case gave their first opportunity for a mass appeal—Sacco and Vanzetti were martyrs of the proletariat, murdered by reactionaries trying to preserve an unjust social order. As Eugene Lyons wrote in his book, *The Life and Death of Sacco and Vanzetti:* "They were sacrificed to the basic fears of capitalist society. They died for the working class of the world."

Seen from this point of view two alien Reds could expect no justice from a Massachusetts court or a Dedham jury. That jury had obviously not debated long over the case, for it took them only five hours to bring in their verdict.

During my month in Dedham I couldn't help but wonder about that earlier jury. Drawn in much the same way that we were, they couldn't have been so very different from ourselves. And what were we? Some middle-class, some working-class, a few of us stupid, a few opinionated, but most of us reasonable enough to weigh an issue. At least we tried to overcome our prejudices; we felt it on our conscience that we should be fair. The jury I sat on would have been prejudiced against Reds, but they would not have convicted a Communist on a capital charge because of his political beliefs. It didn't seem to me the Sacco-Vanzetti jury could have been otherwise. Granted even that the foreman was prejudiced, there would have been some of the others who would have stood out against injustice. I felt sure that when the jury decided that Sacco and Vanzetti were guilty, it was because they were convinced that they were guilty of murder.

Thinking of the great trial I found myself wondering how I should have voted if I had been on the Sacco-Vanzetti jury, knowing little or nothing of the background of the case but merely faced with what was offered me day after day in six weeks of testimony. As soon as I had the time I went back to the transcript of the trial itself. If there was any answer to this question, it would be there.

There was much that the transcript could not offer —the actuality of the past moment, the atmosphere of the court with its tensions, the appearance of the witnesses and the defendants, the subtleties that could be gathered from a tone of voice but could not be preserved in black and white. Yet the substance, the prime matter of the trial endured, each word spoken during that six weeks pressed and dried between the now yellowing pages. Over 2,000 pages of testimony faced me, with the repetitions, the irrelevancies, the long-drawn-out legal impasses that I had become all too familiar with as a juror—and then the sudden revelation of the living fact from the dead record. One hundred and sixty-seven witnesses there were, including the ballistics experts.

Through the long days of another summer I occupied myself with this inchoate mass that gradually took shape and form as I read. I tried to disavow any preconceptions, to imagine myself in the jury box at Dedham occupied solely with the question of whether two men murdered two other men, and knowing no more about it in advance than the evidence offered. How should I have judged?

I knew one thing anyway—that I should have disregarded the experts. My month had taught me that. Experts canceled each other out as the paid bias of either side, and a jury then decided on other grounds. The real grounds in this case were the half dozen or so witnesses who identified Sacco—and to a lesser extent Vanzetti—as being at or near the scene of the murder on that April day. In opposition to them were an equal number of witnesses who testified that these two were not the men. It was a question finally of which group to believe. Every witness who saw the get-away car testified there were five men in it. The weakest part of the Commonwealth's case was that it made no effort to account for the remaining three, as Ehrmann did in his book. And the prosecution never did establish an adequate motive for the crime.

On the other hand Sacco and Vanzetti were both armed the night the police picked them up, Sacco

CONTINUED ON PAGE 109

In The Passion of Sacco and Vanzetti *Shahn imagined the Lowell Committee—left to right, Robert Grant, A. Lawrence Lowell, and Samuel W. Stratton—standing near the coffins of the cobbler and the fish peddler with Judge Thayer raising an approving hand in the background. His opponents felt that Lowell's Yankee background prejudiced him against the two anarchists, yet during the "Red scare" of the twenties he had defended Harvard professors accused of radicalism.*

When American colonists sorely needed
friends, a Dutch island governor risked
political ruin by saluting the rebels' flag

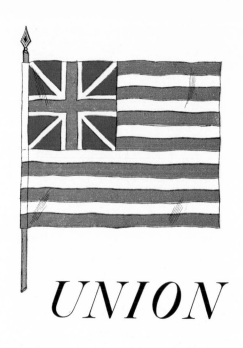

ELEVEN GUNS
for the GRAND UNION

By PHILLIPS MELVILLE

*Johannes de Graaff, gover-
nor of St. Eustatius, boldly
returned the* Andrew Do-
ria's *salute. In this portrait,
copied in 1837 from an
original owned by the De
Graaff family, he holds the
dispatch informing him of
the signing of the Decla-
ration of Independence.*

Summer was on the wane in wartime Philadelphia, 1776, and the city which had startled the world with the Declaration of Independence was alive with purposeful activity. To John Trottman, age seventeen and on vacation from the college at Princeton, its bustle and excitement were in welcome contrast to the quiet atmosphere of his home in Barbados.

During his stay in America, Trottman's guardians were theoretically the Messrs. James & Dunker, Philadelphia merchants; but these gentlemen were too deeply engrossed in more pressing affairs to pay much attention to their ward. Or perhaps they were just indulgent where he was concerned. In any case, he was allowed to roam the city of Philadelphia in the company of his friend George West of Carolina.

One late September afternoon, the boys were exploring the water front, their attention absorbed by vessels discharging their varied cargoes or by shipyards such as that of Wharton & Humphreys, where the first warships of the infant American Navy had been converted from merchantmen less than a year earlier. Whatever the attraction, they lingered until dark in a locale which held considerable danger for able-bodied young men.

Before they were aware of what was happening, a group of rough characters materialized out of the gloom, barring their way. A few abrupt questions and the lads were suddenly seized and forcibly propelled in the direction of an empty wharf. There they were tumbled into a ship's longboat, where a hard fist or belaying pin could discourage any outcry they might make. After an hour of steady rowing, a vessel loomed dark at anchor in the river, and waiting hands hauled them aboard.

Thus, somewhat unceremoniously, John Trottman and George West entered the service of the Continental Navy aboard the brigantine *Andrew Doria,* Captain Isaiah Robinson commanding. Then lying at Gloucester, New Jersey, awaiting orders from the Marine Committee of Congress, the vessel on which Trottman and West found themselves had some claim to distinction. Supposedly named for the great admiral of the Genoese republic, Andrea Doria, she was nevertheless referred to—in diplomatic and intelligence reports and by those who served aboard her— as *Andrew Doria.* She was one of several assorted craft purchased the preceding year as a nucleus of the new Navy, and in the conversion to a ship of war her sides and bulwarks had been reinforced, with the latter pierced for fourteen guns. The crew consisted of 130 officers and men, including 30 marines. Details of the ship's construction are lacking, but it was reportedly similar to that of the *Cabot,* another of the converted vessels, which was 75 feet long on deck, 25 feet abeam.

Captain Nicholas Biddle had been the *Andrew Doria*'s first commander, and he had taken her on the raid on Nassau in March, 1776, as part of Commodore Esek Hopkins' small fleet. The ship had suffered minor damage in an indecisive engagement with the frigate *Glasgow* off Block Island in April; then had made three short cruises, capturing ten prizes, of which two were transports loaded with British troops. Returning to the Delaware from his last cruise, Captain Biddle anchored off Chester, Pennsylvania, on September 17, 1776, and shortly thereafter placed the brigantine in a shipyard for refitting. Here Biddle left the *Andrew Doria* to assume command of the frigate *Randolph,* which was nearing completion.

Captain Isaiah Robinson was thus newly in command, busily engaged in organizing and manning the brigantine, fresh from overhaul. Under the circumstances he was probably glad to have as his first lieutenant Joshua Barney, who had received his commission in the Navy at the hand of Robert Morris. Barney had served with Robinson aboard the *Sachem,* and at seventeen he was already an experienced ship's officer and a veteran of sea warfare.

The skipper of the *Doria* was, however, having trouble completing his crew. It was almost impossible to induce experienced seamen to serve aboard warships of the Continental Navy, where discipline was more severe, the term of enlistment longer, and the prospect for prize money appreciably less than aboard privateers. It should not be assumed, however, that Captain Robinson had sent out a press gang to fill his urgent need. This form of recruiting was in the hands of water-front gangs who deemed it their patriotic duty to supply the Continental Navy with needed hands. There was grim humor in waylaying known or suspected Tories and delivering them aboard Navy ships to serve, perforce, the cause they opposed. It could be profitable, too, for it would be naïve to imagine that the victims arrived aboard ship with anything left in their pockets.

On October 17 the Marine Committee wrote Robinson, informing him that he was to make a voyage under orders from the Secret Committee of Congress. On this mission he was to collect and transmit useful intelligence; take good care of the *Andrew Doria,* her supplies, and equipment; maintain good discipline among his crew, while using them well; treat any prisoners he might take with "tenderness and humanity"; and upon his return deposit a copy of his log and journal with the Marine Committee. Orders from the Secret Committee reached him soon afterwards. They are not in the records, but other references and the course of events reveal their substance.

On October 23 Captain Robinson hove anchor and dropped down the Delaware. After clearing the capes without incident, and with no enemy topsails in sight, the *Doria*'s skipper went below to consult his secret orders. He discovered that he was to proceed to St. Eustatius in the West Indies and there take aboard a cargo of supplies for the Continental Army. He was also to perform the diplomatic mission of delivering a copy of the Declaration of Independence to the governor of this Dutch possession. The destination and purpose of his voyage now clear, Robinson set a course for the Leeward Islands.

The quality of the service rendered by those reluctant seamen Trottman and West during the voyage south is not recorded. We have a clue, however, in an affidavit subsequently made by Trottman, in which he said that "he was treated by everyone as well as he could expect, under the circumstances, except by the boatsman [sic], a foreigner, who beat him several times." This would be normal in those days, and one may sympathize with a seasoned bosun exasperated by a "college young gentleman" unaccustomed to jump at the word of command. The experience probably did Trottman little harm, but it certainly failed to inspire him with enthusiasm for the Revolutionary cause, for a naval career, or for the *Andrew Doria*.

The island of St. Eustatius, then better known as Statia, is a small spot on the chart about 125 nautical miles southeast of St. Thomas in the Virgin Islands. Roughly triangular, about nine square miles in area, it has as a principal feature the Quill, an extinct crater that rises abruptly to 1,950 feet at its extreme eastern end. There is no harbor, but along its southern shore is a splendid roadstead in which as many as 200 vessels may lie sheltered from the easterly trades. The town of Oranjestad is at the foot of the Quill, between it and a bluff 80 to 100 feet high that overlooks a long, narrow beach fronting the roadstead. At the edge of the bluff before the town stands Fort Oranje. Before the American Revolution the population of the island did not exceed 150 white persons and 1,200 Negroes, most of them engaged in raising sugar.

The outbreak of war brought a startling change to Statia. With the British blockading the North American coast, the bulk of Europe's trade with the American colonies was diverted to the West Indies. There cargoes were either transferred to American vessels to run the blockade or stored pending the outcome of the war, since rising prices would assure profits. No other place in that part of the world afforded such advantages of location and spacious anchorage; and of even greater importance was the fact that the Dutch States General had proclaimed it a free port where all were welcome regardless of nationality. As a result, Statia became the preferred sanctuary whither foreign cargoes might be brought and traded under the protection of Dutch neutrality.

An already active commerce received additional impetus when France entered the war, making ports in the British and French possessions liable to attack. Leading merchants of both these nationalities removed their activities to St. Eustatius, which became the principal trading center in the West Indies. Here goods might be assembled and stored, secure from seizure or destruction by the enemy. Here a merchant might deal with American agents, and not a few British citizens succumbed to the temptation of this profitable *sub rosa* trade with their country's foes.

To accommodate the tremendous volume of trade, a double row of warehouses was constructed along the beach below the fort, extending for nearly a mile and a half. The population of the island expanded proportionately, and by 1780 it is reported to have exceeded 30,000 persons—more than Boston could claim at the time.

Statia soon became the major source of European goods and manufactures for the rebellious colonies, as well as a channel through which they obtained gunpowder, ammunition, and other military supplies. The traffic in munitions had to be disguised, of course, in view of Dutch neutrality, but the importance of Statia to the American cause cannot be overemphasized.

It is hardly surprising that the Dutch traders were partial toward the authors of their increasing prosperity. They had a natural sympathy for a struggle for independence such as the Dutch Republic already enjoyed, and the governor of St. Eustatius had shown such a marked favoritism for American interests that the British government made a formal protest. In consequence, the governor had been recalled to Holland in July of 1776, and his secretary, Johannes de Graaff, was appointed in his stead.

A man of marked administrative ability and business acumen, De Graaff was also a skillful lawyer. He quickly attained a dominant position, not only because of his official status, but also by reason of personal wealth, for he owned several plantations, held mortgages on others, and is said to have owned or held an interest in sixteen vessels trading between Statia and Europe.

Such was the local situation when the *Andrew Doria* made her landfall three weeks after leaving the Delaware. Pausing long enough to snap up a couple of prizes in the vicinity, the vessel swept past the Quill into the roadstead before Oranjestad, the Grand Union ensign waving proudly at her gaff. Captain Robinson was determined that his arrival should be observed, and he selected an anchorage directly before Fort Oranje. Rounding into the wind, topsails aback, the brigantine slowed to a stop and then began to gather sternway. At this moment her anchor was let go, her sails clewed up and furled, and up to her main truck went a Dutch standard. Another Grand Union was run up at the fore, and a staff bearing a navy jack was raised on her bowsprit cap. Then, all being in readiness, the first shot of a thirteen-gun national salute resounded through the anchorage.

As the American warship came to anchor, Abraham Ravené, commandant of Fort Oranje, caused the Dutch flag to be dipped, as was customary. The *Andrew Doria*'s gun salute, however, created a problem he was not prepared to cope with. He realized that a return salute would signify official recognition of the sovereignty of the nation whose flag was thus honored, and since the flag in this case was that of Great Britain's rebellious colonies, an answering salute would connote Dutch recognition of their independence. British ships were present in the roads, and news of the affair would speedily reach British officialdom.

Foreseeing serious consequences, Ravené prudently sought out Governor de Graaff to obtain instructions. The Governor was evidently aware of the arrival of the American vessel and of her salute, which would have been visible from his estate at Concordia. And he promptly replied, "Fire a return salute with two guns less than for a national salute." Hastening back to the fort, Ravené put this order into execution, rehoisted the Dutch flag, and fired eleven "honor shots" in reply to the American thirteen.

Governor de Graaff could not have been ignorant of the Declaration of Independence. Samuel Curzon, local agent for the Continental Congress, would have kept him informed of developments in Philadelphia. Possibly De Graaff suspected the formality of the

The Andrew Doria, *flying the Grand Union ensign at her fore and stern, receives the salute of Fort Oranje. Once ashore, wrote an American agent, her skipper was "most graciously received" by the governor, who expressed "the greatest desire and Intention to protect a trade with us here." This and the painting on page 63 were done for this article by the author.*

61

Andrew Doria's arrival and, realizing that the official presentation of the Declaration would place him in an unequivocal position, arrived at a quick compromise. By authorizing a return with two guns less than the national salute, he made certain that an honor would be rendered, thus pleasing the Americans. On the other hand, should he be called to account for his bold action, the nature of his return salute would allow him to call it a courtesy, not signifying recognition of American independence.

The exchange of salutes created an immediate and understandable stir in Oranjestad and aboard the ships in the roadstead, where the implications of the affair were well understood. Everywhere it was agreed that the British would soon hear of it and react emphatically. As chance had it, the vessel to starboard of the *Andrew Doria* was a sloop from the nearby British island of St. Christopher, or St. Kitts. Aboard her were a gentleman named James Fraser and two British captains, John Dean and John Spicer. The trio had been on deck preparing to go ashore as the *Doria* rounded the Quill. Catching sight of her, Fraser exclaimed, "There comes the tender of a man-o-war," meaning a small vessel that frequently cruised in company with a frigate or larger ship. "No, by G—d!" Dean replied, "She's an American privateer,—for do you not see the flag of the Continental Congress with thirteen stripes?" They continued to watch as the *Doria* anchored and fired her salute, and immediately afterward they entered their boat and pulled for shore. They had not reached the landing place when the return salute was fired by the fort. Ashore, they found the exchange of salutes the main topic of conversation in the inns and grog shops and noted an air of elation among the Americans and their friends. When they completed the business that had brought them to Statia, Fraser and his two companions returned to their sloop and set sail for St. Kitts, where they related the saluting incident to the authorities.

It is quite possible that they were not the first to arrive with the news. This distinction may belong to young John Trottman, who reached St. Kitts at seven o'clock in the morning on November 17. On the evening of the preceding day, Captain Robinson, back aboard his brigantine after paying his official call on the Governor, had himself rowed to an American pilot boat anchored in the roads. Going aboard, he directed the crew of his gig to return to the *Doria*. The boat crew consisted of four men, of whom Trottman was one.

As they made their way back in the gathering darkness, Trottman perceived an opportunity to escape from his enforced service. Resting on his oar, he proposed that they head for St. Kitts, looming dimly eight miles away to the southeast. Persuaded by promises of reward or disenchanted with life in the Continental Navy, his companions agreed, and the boat was headed toward the British island. It took them all night to make it, but shortly after sunrise they landed at Sandy Point and were soon recounting their experiences aboard the *Andrew Doria*, the purpose of her visit to St. Eustatius, and the events of the preceding day.

While Christer Greathead, president of St. Christopher and Nevis, was digesting the information that Trottman, Fraser, Dean, Spicer, *et al.* had brought him, another event provided a second painful jolt to British sensibilities. On November 21 the *Baltimore Hero*, an American privateer alleged to have been outfitted at St. Eustatius and owned, in part, by Maryland's enterprising agent, Abraham van Bibber, sailed out of the anchorage at Statia and waylaid a British brigantine which had left St. Kitts shortly before. Attacking the Britisher within sight of both islands, but beyond range of the Dutch batteries and thus outside neutral waters, the *Hero* effected an easy capture. A prize crew was placed aboard her with orders to make for the Delaware, whereupon the privateer sailed in triumph back to her former anchorage, the Grand Union proudly spanking the breeze.

The victim of this affair was the *May,* William Taylor master, and the vessel and her cargo were the property of one Fosta M. Connell, a British resident of Dominica. The latter promptly let out a howl that hit the sensitive ear of President Greathead more painfully because "the act of piracy" had taken place under his very nose.

After studying these two episodes as described for him by witnesses and victims, Greathead addressed an emphatic protest to the governor of the neighboring Dutch island. His letter, dated December 17, 1776, couched in the studied and dignified style of the period, is quite lengthy. Beginning with a reminder of the prolonged friendship, based on treaties, that had hitherto existed between the British and Dutch, he expressed regret at the disagreeable duty of having, now, to protest the partiality and support afforded Great Britain's rebellious American subjects by the inhabitants of St. Eustatius. He made broad charges regarding Dutch connivance in the traffic in military supplies and outfitting of privateers, quoting the *Baltimore Hero* as an example. Of the *Andrew Doria* he had this to say:

"Also, that an armed vessel called the *Andrew Doria,* commanded by a Captain Robinson, belonging to and in the service of the before-mentioned rebels, dropped anchor in the roads of St. Eustatius, and

The Doria, *at right, battles H.M.S.* Racehorse *off Puerto Rico on the way back from Statia. The* Doria *defeated and captured the British sloop-of-war, but soon after reaching home she herself was destroyed to prevent her capture by the enemy.*

with hoisted flag, known to be that of the rebels called Continental Congress, did, about the middle of November last, salute with thirteen shots the fortress of her high and mighty the Dutch government, called the Orange fort; and that this salute was afterward answered by that fort with the same solemnity due to the flags of independent sovereign states; and to that ship it was then permitted to take aboard a cargo of gunpowder, other ammunition, and provisions, at St. Eustatius, for the use of the American army."

After further expressions of indignation he added a final presumptuous demand:

"I therefore exact from you, sir . . . a sufficient reason for the offense done to His Majesty's flag by the honor rendered his rebellious subjects by Fort Orange; and I require, also, sir . . . you will not only use your authority to prevent a repetition of such violation of faith, but will employ at the same time immediate means to give complete restitution to the sufferers by the piracy committed by the sloop *Balti-*

more Hero, and that the fellow-helpers and abettors in that act may be discovered, apprehended, and have the merited punishment that will be a terror to others."

To insure prompt attention to his letter, Greathead directed his solicitor general, John Stanley, and a committee to lay the matter before the Dutch governor in person. No doubt President Greathead hoped that Stanley would return with De Graaff's abject apologies and his assurance that the people of Statia would forthwith mend their ways. If so, he was to be sadly disappointed.

Governor de Graaff received Stanley and accepted the letter, but he flatly refused to discuss its contents with the delegation. Instead, he composed a reply, dated December 23, in which he dismissed with commendable brevity the allegations of aid to the American rebels and outfitting of privateers. He pointed out that he could not proceed against alleged offenders except upon "circumstantial proofs founded upon the most authentic information; and that the facts shall be set forth in good order, and ratified with witnesses." Referring to the salute to the *Doria* he said, "I flatter myself that, if my masters exact it, I shall be able to give such an account as will be satisfactory." As to Greathead's presuming to take him to task, he announced that the President's request "seems to bear the appearance of exacting account of actions . . . that no one in the world is entitled to excepting my gentlemen and masters."

On receipt of this, President Greathead undertook a second letter to De Graaff, dated December 26, and couched in considerably milder terms:

"The impartial world will judge between us, whether these honor shots, answered on purpose by a Dutch fort to a rebellious brigantine called the *Andrew Doria*, with a flag known to the commander of that fort as the flag of His Majesty's rebelling subjects, is or is not a partiality in favor of these rebels, and a public offense done to His Majesty's flag. Whether the rebel brigantine fired thirteen or eleven honor shots, and whether they are answered with an equal or inferior number, will not alter, I think, the real ground of my complaint in this regard; nor do I find anything in your letter that contains any denial or disavowal of that fact."

Having done his duty under the circumstances, and perceiving that any further exchange was quite unlikely to produce satisfaction from Governor de Graaff, Greathead assembled copies of the correspondence, carefully enclosed sworn affidavits by all the witnesses, and forwarded them to London for such action as His Majesty's ministers might see fit to take.

While the exchange of letters between governors was going on, the *Andrew Doria* remained at Statia taking on her cargo. At last her hold was full, and early in the spring of 1777 Captain Robinson bade farewell to his friends and set sail for the Delaware. The British had maintained a close watch on the American warship and, aware of her impending departure, sent the sloop *Racehorse*, twelve guns, Lieutenant James Jones commander, to lie in wait along her probable course. The *Doria* had reached a point off the western end of Puerto Rico, when the *Racehorse* was sighted. Captain Robinson cleared for action. In the running fight that followed, the British sloop proved no match for the smartly served, double-reinforced four-pounders of the Continental brigantine, and after two hours of battering, with her commander mortally wounded and a large number of her crew also casualties, the *Racehorse* struck her colors. A prize crew was put aboard and she was successfully brought into the Delaware, where she was soon joined by her captor, which had paused long enough en route to gather in a merchant snow [a square-rigged vessel similar to a brig]. The *Doria* made port without her first lieutenant, however. Barney had volunteered as prize master of the captured snow and sailed away to a series of adventures that rival fiction. He was never to set foot aboard the *Andrew Doria* again.

The British government, on receipt of President Greathead's report, issued a menacing note to The Hague. After an exchange, the States General found it diplomatically expedient to recall De Graaff to Holland to give a firsthand account of affairs at Statia. A full year elapsed before he put in his appearance, but when he did so he defended himself and his administration so ably as to be cleared of all censure. Reinstated in his post at St. Eustatius, he served until February 3, 1781, when retribution finally appeared in the person of Admiral Sir George Rodney with a British fleet. England had finally gone to war with Holland, but Sir George came too late. Statia's role as a vital supply point during the early, critical years of the Revolution had already passed. France had by now come to the aid of the rebels and had tipped the scales of war.

Governor Johannes de Graaff, firm friend of the United States when friends were scarce and sorely needed, is unknown to most Americans and virtually forgotten. No biographer has yet been moved to describe his life. But the tourist who visits Fort Oranje and from its terraced rampart, still lined with ancient cannon, surveys the roadstead where several hundred vessels once rode at anchor, will find a bronze plaque affixed to the wall of the old fort. It reads:

IN COMMEMORATION
OF THE
SALUTE TO THE FLAG OF THE UNITED STATES
FIRED IN THIS FORT ON 16 NOVEMBER 1776
BY ORDER OF
JOHANNES DE GRAAFF
GOVERNOR OF ST. EUSTATIUS
IN REPLY TO A NATIONAL GUN-SALUTE
FIRED BY THE
UNITED STATES BRIG-OF-WAR, ANDREW DORIA
UNDER CAPTAIN ISAIAH ROBINSON
OF THE CONTINENTAL NAVY

———————

HERE THE SOVEREIGNTY OF THE
UNITED STATES OF AMERICA
WAS FIRST FORMALLY ACKNOWLEDGED TO A
NATIONAL VESSEL BY A FOREIGN OFFICIAL
PRESENTED BY FRANKLIN DELANO ROOSEVELT
PRESIDENT OF THE UNITED STATES OF AMERICA

Phillips Melville is a retired Air Force colonel now living in Washington, D.C., who has undertaken a new career as a marine artist and author.

Williamstown Branch

The time is 1898, and the place, a small Vermont town on a branch line railroad. Any resemblance to present-day America is purely accidental, for the Williamstown that R. L. Duffus knew as a boy might just as well be part of another country on a different planet. As we read the veteran newsman's reminiscence of his life sixty years ago (it is fair to assume that he was a typical boy in a typical rural American town), we are likely to feel something beyond mere nostalgia—perhaps a certain regret for a more peaceful, more leisurely, and less impersonal way of life that can never be recaptured.

By R. L. DUFFUS

ILLUSTRATED FOR AMERICAN HERITAGE
BY ARTUR MAROKVIA

VERMONT IN THE 1890's:

A boy's world full of wonder

My father said, one day when I was eight and we were living in Mill Village, that some day he'd hire a horse and rig from J. K. Linton and take us all to see the Barre Quarries. Two years later, when I was ten and we were living in the General E. Bass house, we still hadn't gone to see the quarries, but I kept hoping we would.

The quarries, in the hills above Barre and maybe four miles from Williamstown, were the source of the granite industry in that part of Vermont. In my eyes they were among the marvels of the world, even unseen. Of course we saw in many ways the traces and effects of this primeval rock. From Graniteville a branch railroad wound down to Barre, but there was also a steep dirt road descending into Williamstown. Down this road, in some of my earliest memories, came the great stone-laden wagons, brakes making sparks at the last steep pitch into our valley, horses holding hard back, the drivers sometimes standing, reins tight in hand, and swearing blue blazes, and loving the admiration they drew from us boys.

I thought of Barre Quarries as a distant journey, though they were in fact no further away than places to which we often went on our bicycles. Not as far away, really, as Barre itself. But I wouldn't have dreamed of going there alone, and somehow it never occurred to a group of us to ride our bicycles up there.

This may have been partly because the quarries, even then, were two hundred feet down and our parents feared their boys might go too near the edge and fall in; or be too near when a blast went off and get blown back home in small pieces; or be mashed under a few tons of granite. The Barre Quarries seemed distant because they were strange and dangerous, wonderful, legendary and romantic.

So Barre Quarries represented to me, at the time I was ten years old, the spirit of travel and adventure. When I say this I do not mean to imply that Williamstown, even then, with only dirt roads leading to and from it and with only one rickety branch railroad line, was shut away like a dream village in a fairy story.

Williamstown people traveled, all right. One Williamstown boy had become a well-known war correspondent and gone all over the world and been shot at; we boys envied him, though we never saw him. A Williamstown man who had accumulated some modest means—perhaps by selling timberland to people from

outside the state who didn't know too much about local timber and terrain—made an extensive trip one year. Williamstown people with less money could go on excursions to Boston or Montreal for about ten dollars for the round trip.

The Central Vermont Railway of that day did all it possibly could to make a passenger realize he was traveling. It shot soot in through the open windows; it rolled and rocked going around curves; it backed and switched in Barre and Montpelier; it came down to the main line at Montpelier Junction and let everybody stand half an hour or so on a windy platform waiting for the train to come roaring down from Northfield and points south; in fact, there wasn't anything that railroad wouldn't do to make a small boy contented.

I didn't readily start conversations with strangers, but I heard the commercial travelers called drummers talking in J. K. Linton's store and at the Monument House. They had grand airs, as men naturally would who had been around so much. They knew the world, and nothing could fool them—no siree, as they used to say. They weren't the sort who would blow out the gas when they put up at a fashionable city hotel, and as for tall buildings, they had seen them all—even in some cases the Flatiron Building and Madison Square Garden in New York City—and thought nothing of it.

And there were other sorts of travelers, stranger ones than the drummers, who, after all, just traveled up and down the state of Vermont selling groceries or patent medicines or things like that to storekeepers.

There were the pack peddlers, for example. I still remember one of these—or is this memory a combination of several peddlers? Anyhow, he had come to our door and my mother had let him in, and he had opened his pack, well wrapped in oil cloth, on the kitchen table. I think there were fabrics of some sort, for I have an impression of soft colors and my mother fingering the stuff with the evident thought of making a dress or apron, perhaps for my shiny-eyed younger sister, who was standing by.

But what stuck in my memory was something else: the bright packages of needles, thimbles, knives of various shapes and sizes—jackknives among them, I think; indeed, maybe this was the peddler who sold my mother the pocketknife I treasured so long and which made a scar I still carry on the little finger of my left hand.

I don't suppose I ever even spoke a word to a gypsy.

FROM *Williamstown Branch* BY R. L. DUFFUS, PUBLISHED BY
W. W. NORTON & COMPANY, INC. © 1958 BY R. L. DUFFUS.

One reason was the usual one of shyness, together with the belief that they probably didn't speak English at all but some outlandish language of their own. Another reason was that gypsies were suspected of kidnaping children, carrying them off, and bringing them up in their turn to be gypsies and kidnap other children.

One lot of them camped one spring or summer night between the General E. Bass house and the Pool Bridge. They had horses and gaily painted wagons and carts; their women were in bright colors, with much jewelry and handkerchiefs over their heads; even their menfolk were picturesque with earrings and sashes. No doubt their business was horse-trading and no doubt they traded some. But for me they had again the immense allurement of people who had no abiding homes but traveled wherever they wanted to, all over the face of the earth.

Even if I didn't talk to them, I could walk by them slowly, and look at them, and come back after a while and take another look. Their camping arrangements were simple. They didn't have to have hot and cold running water, the way they would now; nobody had hot and cold running water then, except President Mc-Kinley, Queen Victoria, and J. P. Morgan, and I wasn't sure even about them. And their other sanitary needs were easily taken care of, in that free generation and place, when sanitation wasn't even a word we knew. So they unhitched their horses and let them graze beside the road, which was the property of anybody that

wanted it and it didn't require permission if a horse wished to graze beside it.

I didn't want to be kidnaped by a gypsy, and I was not. But I did keep thinking, as I saw this encampment, and especially as I smelled what the gypsies were cooking in iron pots over open fires, What would it be like to be kidnaped by gypsies and grow up and be, to all intents and purposes, a gypsy?

The next best thing to the gypsies that came to Williamstown, and that kept alive in me the spirit of travel and adventure, were the Uncle Tom shows and an occasional vaudeville show that played for a night in the Town Hall.

The Uncle Tom shows had a good deal besides Uncle Tom, Little Eva, and Simon Legree and one or more Lawyers Marks. They had a horse or two, sometimes an elephant, sometimes a man who walked a tightrope and did tricks on it, once in a while a trapeze performer, and a girl who did something or other and had spangles all over her. Everything that didn't have anything to do with Uncle Tom was called a Sacred Concert, and cost ten cents extra.

I think a small, one-ring circus came to Williamstown at about that time, too, and some boys carried water for the elephant and got a free ticket as a result.

We did get to see the Uncle Tom shows, and maybe a one-ring circus or two in Williamstown—but I am puzzled about this, because my recollections are scrambled. I suppose one might say this was one manner of traveling; one didn't go all over the world, to Barre Quarries, and Burlington, and Quebec, and China and such places, but the flavor and smell of the far-off rolled in upon us under the big tents, and it was as if Williamstown had removed itself, for a night, to Burlington or Chicago or China, or one of those places.

A few traveling vaudeville shows came through, too, and did somewhat the same thing, only they were not quite so glamorous. Before I left Williamstown these shows usually carried a few reels of film and a motion picture projector, and we thought this was wonderful and in many ways better than the magic lanterns we had at home.

But what I recall of the vaudeville shows was chiefly the girls or women who kicked up their heels and danced and sang. There was one who had red ruffles under her dress, practically all the way down to her knees but no further, and I wondered if I ought to look at them.

My father repeated that some day he would hire a rig from the livery stable and take the whole family to the Barre Quarries. He might as well have said that he would hire a rig and take us to San Francisco or Bombay. My father never took us to the Barre Quarries. His health broke first, we children went away for our schooling after we had passed through the Williamstown Graded School, and that was the end of that.

Before I saw the Barre Quarries for the first time I had crossed and recrossed the United States as far as San Francisco and the Pacific; my father had gone to California, where he died; my mother, too, was dead; the rest of the family was scattered geographically, though united by common affections, memories, and experiences.

Twenty-one years after the year to which these memories and experiences at the moment tether me, I took my wife to Vermont. That was 1919. The granite sheds were no longer operating in Williamstown. Of the recollections of my childhood there survived the Williamstown Branch of the Central Vermont, soon to be abandoned; the Monument House or its successor; the J. K. Linton store, which had become a farmers' co-operative; and the General E. Bass house.

The automobile had not captured all the roads, especially not the side roads. I said to my wife, "Let's hire a rig at the livery stable and go up and look at the quarries." So we hired a rig at the livery stable and went up and looked at the quarries.

I was glad enough I had waited for my father to take the family there, even though he had never been able to do so.

But I was sorry for him, to whom it made no difference any more, that he had never been able to lay his hands on quite enough money.

Williamstown Branch

I never heard him called anything but Old Man Webb, though he must have had a first name, and maybe a middle name. I never heard anybody mention his relatives. If he had had a wife, she was certainly dead when I knew Mr. Webb. If he had children, they may have been, as we often said, out west somewhere, but they certainly weren't around Williamstown.

Mr. Webb, when I knew him, if I can truly say that a boy of ten could then or at any other time really know a venerable engineer on the Central Vermont Railway, lived in the Monument House. Hotel rates in small Vermont towns in 1898 must have been low enough to permit steadily employed workmen to board and room there. I wouldn't be surprised if Mr. Webb paid as much as six dollars a week or as little as four dollars a week.

Mr. Webb's locomotive was a bell-stacked, wood-burning affair of the sort seen in pictures of the Civil War. For all I know, this very locomotive may have fought in the Civil War. Its fuel was chunks of wood derived from a woodpile under a big shed beside the tracks between the freight shed and the feed store.

When he got to his engine in the fairly early morning, the fireman would already have steam up. All Mr. Webb had to do was to climb into the cab, sink down into a luxuriously padded leather seat, and open the throttle. He would then back up to the baggage car and coach, or maybe half coach and half baggage car, that made up his train, wait for Conductor Jim Kennealy to give him the signal, and go tooting away to Barre.

Mr. Webb would descend the grade to Barre, back up into Barre station as his schedule required, unhitch his passenger coach and baggage equipment, and spend the day switching in the Barre yards. When his switching was over he would reattach his coach and baggage cars, or car, and go home, up the grade, to Williamstown. He arrived there, I presume, around half past seven in the evening.

In the meantime another train would come up from Montpelier, this time with a coal-burning engine with a small stack, pick up passengers who desired to go out into the big world, and proceed with them first to Barre, then to Montpelier Junction. At Montpelier Junction the passengers changed to the main line of the Central Vermont, over which they could go to Burlington via Essex Junction, or, better yet, to Montreal and the West. With this afternoon train you could scoot clear out of Vermont. With Mr. Webb you were sure of getting home.

But though I did want to be an engineer, pulling on a throttle and watching the world go by, I hardly expected to run an engine as far as Montpelier Junction, let alone Montreal. I was, in my way, a modest boy. I just wanted to be a Mr. Webb. It seemed to me there couldn't be any life a man could reasonably look for that would be better than the one Mr. Webb led.

I am thinking of one episode that might have made Mr. Webb bite off a few of his own whiskers and swallow them. In spite of the fact that the statute of limitations has probably run its course several times over, I shall not mention the names of those involved. I shall not even suggest that my brother was present.

When a locomotive comes to the end of a branch line it must do one of two things: it must find a way to turn round or it must back up. In Williamstown, as at the terminals of other branch lines, this problem was solved by a simple device called a turntable.

This turntable worked by muscle power. Mr. Webb would drive his engine carefully upon it, taking pains not to keep on into the adjacent swamp. Then the fireman—never, I believe, Mr. Webb—would apply himself to a long lever and walk the engine round until its cowcatcher was where its rear end had been. Mr. Webb would make sure that the turntable track and the railroad track were locked in the correct positions, and then he would drive his engine off again.

This process was a miracle that happened twelve times a week, counting both trains into and out of Williamstown and not counting Sundays, but with myself and my young friends it never grew stale. We watched with bugged-out eyes whenever we had a chance, and

we hoped that some day Mr. Webb would invite us into the cab while the miracle was being performed.

The next best thing was to wait till Mr. Webb and other employees of the Central Vermont Railway were out of sight or busy at something else that kept them looking the other way, and then operate that turntable ourselves, though with no engine.

In addition to the rails provided for the locomotive, the turntable had rails to turn on. It was, one might say, a sort of circular railway. Any reader who lived in Williamstown, Vermont, in 1898 could figure it out for himself. If a boy can get his hands on a thing like a turntable, as we did, he is sooner or later going to run that turntable off its track. And this we did—myself and whoever was hanging around with me that day.

I don't know how we did this, for this turntable must have been built to stand wear and tear. At all events, it gave a shudder, a groan, and a hollow clatter and stuck tight, about halfway round. We worked at it a while, growing uneasy because it was about time for Mr. Webb to pull in from Barre, and usually he turned his locomotive around before supper instead of after breakfast.

As I have mentioned, Mr. Webb was in the habit of bringing his train in on time. On this particular day he was three-quarters of an hour late because he had had to wait for a carload of guano fertilizer that was coming in from Boston on the main line. Mr. Seaver, the feed store proprietor, had been making a fuss about this guano, which stank to high heaven but did make things grow when properly applied.

Mr. Webb felt that fate had been unkind, first in this delay, second, because he had to take time to set out the car of guano at Mr. Seaver's loading platform, where Mr. Seaver could get at it in the morning.

Mr. Webb therefore arrived in Williamstown hungrier than usual, madder than usual, and fully aware that the supper he was about to get at the Monument House wouldn't be as good or as cheerfully served as it would have been earlier.

I had come upstreet after supper, a criminal returning to the scene. Or almost to the scene, for I hung around J. K. Linton's store, waiting for the whistle. Eight o'clock came, and then quarter after eight, and I now knew that my parents would be wondering where I was—or, assuming that my big brother was also upstreet, where we both were.

The wail of Mr. Webb's manfully struggling locomotive came at last, from down the line a mile or so, near the Tud Holler one-room school building.

I wanted to go home, yet I was curious as to what would happen. It seemed best not to wait. If I were the kind of boy who went home in the evening as his bedtime drew near I would be less likely to be suspected as a member of a gang that went around wrecking railroad turntables.

My mother asked me what I had been doing and I said I had been hanging around J. K. Linton's store. My father looked up from his newspaper and said there might be better things to do, and my mother said that if I never went to any worse place than J. K. Linton's store I'd be safe enough. My father said that when he was a boy of ten he was already working out of school hours and tired enough at eight o'clock to be glad to have a chance to go to bed, and not hang around anybody's store. My mother said times had changed, and my father commented that they evidently had.

I lay awake for an hour or so, or maybe fifteen minutes, for lying awake was something I wasn't used to. In the morning, I had my breakfast, still in a worried frame of mind and not sure—indeed, I am not yet sure—whether my brother or others of my young associates were also worried.

I thought it would be best to look into the situation,

but in a cautious way that would not arouse suspicion. I therefore strolled, nonchalantly, so I hoped, toward the J. K. Linton store, then slid round the corner and looked toward the station.

The two cars that were to make up the early train to Barre that morning were still standing beside the station platform. This was unusual, for it was by now nearly nine o'clock, and Mr. Webb should have pulled out an hour and a half before.

Going a little farther around the corner of the store and gazing past Fred Ainsworth's drugstore, I observed that Mr. Webb's locomotive was down by the turntable, a few hundred feet south of the station and therefore to my right.

At the turntable itself there seemed to be quite a group of men, working and arguing, and Mr. Webb, whose upper portion was leaning out of the engine cab, was almost visibly swearing. A man couldn't make the gestures Mr. Webb was making and still be talking in Sunday school language.

I then realized the dismaying truth. Mr. Webb hadn't turned his engine around the night before. He hadn't found out that anything was wrong with the turntable until he had tried to turn the thing around in the morning; or until his current fireman, who was sometimes trusted with the operation, had tried to do so.

Then he had found himself stuck, and his plans for the day had immediately gone wrong. Mr. Webb was going to be so late into Barre that he wouldn't have time for a nap and would be lucky if he had a few minutes in which to eat the slice of steak, the fried potatoes, the thick slices of buttered bread, and the apple pie with which the Monument House had probably provided him.

Mr. Webb was annoyed. He was listening to loud advice from the men struggling with the turntable and was giving even louder advice in return. Nobody seemed to be getting anywhere.

As a normal boy I longed to go over and watch the fun —and listen to it. As a criminal interfering with the Central Vermont Railway and possibly also with the United States mails, I judged I had better not do this.

I ducked over past the station on the north side, out

of sight of any possibly suspicious eye among those struggling with the turntable, scrambled up a sand-bank, and found myself with some of my fellow criminals in the grass at the top.

We watched the animated scene below. One of my companions suddenly drew a long breath. "He's going to back the train down to Barre," said this young man. "Judas Priest! Why didn't he think of that before?"

And this was indeed what that man of brawn and genius, Mr. Webb, actually did. He came away from the turntable with a whooshing of steam and spinning of wheels, picked up his abandoned tender, now well stocked with elm and maple chunks, hitched the front end of his engine to the train, blew his whistle as though he were letting out one last cuss word, and departed for Barre.

In the afternoon a small wrecking train came up from Barre and straightened out the turntable. The four or five men who operated this train were not mad at anybody, because that was what they were paid for and it did not make them late for dinner to fix our turntable. In addition, they did not know one boy from another and did not care who had caused the damage.

We boys kept clear of Mr. Webb and everybody else connected with the Central Vermont Railway for some days after this incident. I thought maybe Mr. Webb would tell our parents and make life difficult for us, but evidently he didn't.

My father looked at my brother and myself rather suspiciously one evening. "They had quite a lot of trouble with the turntable," he observed. "Somebody must have been fooling with it, they think." He paused. "If you were a little bigger I'd wonder if you boys weren't mixed up in it."

"They can't do all the wrong things that get done," said my mother gently.

I didn't say anything, nor did my brother.

"People missed connections all the way to Montreal," my father continued. He went on for a while with his dinner, and I could see, pretending all the while not to watch his expression, that his thoughts were drifting. He held his fork suspended for a mo-ment. "Would you boys like to go to Montreal some day?" he asked.

I imagine we both gasped, as did my sister—his real favorite among us—who was not included in this suggestion.

"Montreal!" I said.

"Maybe," replied my father. "But keep away from that turntable after this. Understand?"

We went exploring one lazy May day down along the tracks toward Barre. There were bare wooden trestles at one or two places, and if we wanted to be brave we would walk them, shuddering courageously at the depths below. I suppose people in authority thought the Williamstown Branch was to be a permanent institution, for once in a while they would send along a few gravel cars and fill in underneath some of these trestles. I wish I had the money they spent doing this; if any of them are still alive they may wish so, too.

Somehow the afternoon went by faster than we thought. It was a good afternoon, with the sun sinking at last behind the West Hill but leaving a good deal of light behind it for a half an hour and more. We started home as it went down, walking slowly along the track and pretending we were railway trains. We could still do this, even though the Central Vermont Railway no longer loved us.

We hadn't got more than halfway home, still following the track, when we heard a whistle behind us. It could be nothing less than Mr. Webb bringing up the evening train, tooting and puffing as he came up the grade, with the fireman ringing the bell and having fun at every cowpath that crossed the rails.

We got off the track as Mr. Webb and his locomotive approached. There was plenty of time to do this, for Mr. Webb was not coming very fast. I suspect he was prolonging the sensation of being about to finish his day's work and get something to eat. And anyhow, the ancient wood-burner he was operating couldn't get up the grade at much more than seven miles an hour. The snorting and puffing it made as it climbed the steeper slopes made me want to get behind and push.

But Mr. Webb wasn't worried. Mr. Webb, as in some sudden flash of insight we all realized, wasn't even mad.

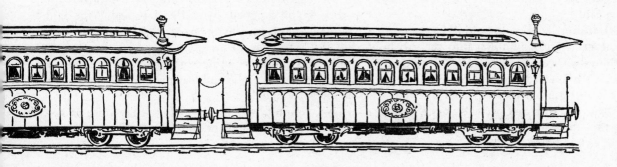

Mr. Webb had had a good day, whatever that meant to him. He saw us as the train approached. We were in a sandbank from which we could not readily escape, though we had plenty of room to let the train go safely by.

Mr. Webb leaned far out of his cab window and relieved himself of more tobacco spit than I would have thought any man outside of a circus would have been capable of. Then he gazed at us fixedly, and I wondered if a sheriff or some other species of policeman wasn't riding with him and getting ready to arrest us.

And then Mr. Webb winked. He winked a wink that began well up in his forehead and ended in a twitch along the left side of his nose.

We looked at each other, the three of us—or maybe that day it was four—and then let out a delighted and simultaneous whoop. Mr. Webb was our friend again; that was what that spitting and winking meant.

Just the same, when we came up to the station, where the brakeman and station agent had just finished unloading the baggage and express, I was a little shy as I walked slowly past the locomotive. The other boys, as I believe, disappeared altogether. At any rate, I was alone as I came up to where Mr. Webb was standing on the apron between the locomotive and the tender.

"Well, Robbie," he said, and I stopped as though I'd been seized by the collar. "I've missed you lately. You haven't been sick, have you?"

I said I hadn't, and he grinned.

"You must watch for the train when you're on the track," Mr. Webb continued. "It ain't a big engine but it would chew up a small boy if it hit him." He motioned. "We're going to turn her round, seeing there's time to do it tonight. Would you like to climb up and help?" He waited, as if I would have to think this one over.

"You're mighty spry," said Mr. Webb. I was—I was already in the cab.

"Uh-huh," I answered. I was breathing hard, not so much with the exertion of jumping into the cab beside Mr. Webb as with the excitement of being there.

"Well, now," Mr. Webb went on, taking his proper seat behind the throttle but leaving room in front of him for me, "you set down and pretend you're the engineer. Take that throttle in your hand—it won't bite you. It only bites bad boys."

I took hold of the lever, feeling Mr. Webb's strong hand beside mine.

"All right," commanded Mr. Webb. "Pull back on it."

I did this, aided and restrained, I suppose, by the engineer. The old locomotive breathed deeply, snorted, and then, slowly responding to the throttle, moved toward the turntable.

"Gosh!" I cried.

Mr. Webb laughed. "That's the way I felt, the first time," he said. "Easy there, easy now." I felt my hand go forward again as he closed the throttle and the engine stopped. Mr. Webb gazed at me thoughtfully. "This turntable is what you might call a delicate apparatus," he observed. "It goes off the rails pretty easy. That's why we come up on it gentle, the way we're doing tonight. You take somebody playing with that turntable that don't know how it operates, and chances are they'll do damage to it."

He seemed to wait for me to speak. "Uh-huh," I said.

Mr. Webb was silent while he inched the locomotive upon the turntable, and the fireman, already in his proper post, turned it round.

"Runs like a sewing machine," remarked Mr. Webb, "since that wrecking crew come up the other day and oiled it."

"Uh-huh," I agreed.

We slid down toward the roundhouse where the ancient engine spent its nights.

"It's a tough life, being an engineer," said Mr. Webb as he climbed slowly down. "How old are you, Robbie?"

I told him.

"In eight years you'll be old enough to be a fireman," Mr. Webb continued, inspecting me carefully. "You'll be a good chunk of a boy by that time. What do you want to be when you grow up, anyhow? How much of a damn fool are you?"

"An engineer," I replied breathlessly. "I mean—"

Mr. Webb laughed. "Just like I thought," he said, "solid maple from ear to ear. Well, I'll tell you, Robbie, if you want to be an engineer nobody can say you can't. If I'm still running eight years from now, I'll take you on as fireman and teach you all I know. You'll be sorry, though."

"No, I won't, Mr. Webb." I found my voice at last. "I'm sorry about the turntable. We all are. I won't ever do it again. We all won't."

"Sure," said Mr. Webb encouragingly. "Sure you won't. And so far as I'm concerned, you never did."

"If you'll take me," I went on bravely, "I'd like to be your fireman. I'll exercise and get real strong. I'm going to be an engineer, Mr. Webb—like you."

Mr. Webb came near purring. I'm glad I said this to him, for I suppose it made him feel like a success in the world. What more success can a man have than doing something that makes a boy want to come along in his footsteps?

The stuff that dreams
are made on

If there were not so many other witnesses I should think I dreamed the town I seem to remember. Surely I dreamed part of it, and a part of it was real. What my brother and sister remembered, I did not wholly remember. What I remembered, and have been trying to tell, may never have been wholly in their memories at all.

It is true, however, that the Williamstown we each knew, in our various ways, in 1898 is not there any more. It was the stuff that dreams are made on and it has now been undreamed, and another sort of morning has come other than the mornings we knew.

The town and village as I knew them seemed permanent. I thought, without ever putting the thought into words, that we were fixed in time and place and nothing would ever change very much; we youngsters would never grow up; our parents would never grow old and die; the past and future were stories and make-believe.

Merrill Linton said one day that his father had said, "This town pretty near broke up last year."

I was startled. I asked how a town could break up. I hadn't noticed anything coming loose.

Merrill shook his head wisely. He didn't know the answer. What I now suppose is that this was partly the tail end of the depression of the 1890's, from which the Spanish-American War and, as we Vermonters, big and little, mostly saw it, the noble and wise policies of the Republican party, had helped to lift us.

It may also have been suspected, even then, that it would be better to haul granite by rail into Barre and Montpelier than to lug it by road or rail into Williamstown. What made Williamstown the most prosperous as well as the most cosmopolitan of small towns was the granite business and the people it brought.

Whatever exists seems natural to a boy. It would snow in January and December, and between those months, about midway, there would be a little warmth —too much, sometimes. But the climate wouldn't change, even though Mr. Ainsworth did once remark during a long dry spell that maybe it was the Lord's will never to let it rain again. Nothing would change. Williamstown, Vermont, 1898, was a finished product the way I looked at it, the way all we boys looked at it. Who can ever believe in the future? There isn't any future.

We therefore looked at our town, not knowing much of it was transient; and at the stone-sheds, the particular feature of our town in 1898, not knowing that they would pass like the insubstantial cobwebs of a dream.

A boy does not think of capital investments and the returns thereon, or of what makes business in general go. Our view of stone-sheds was a material one. There stood the buildings, where our parents would rather we did not go during working hours except when sometimes we took my father's dinner pail to him. There was, during those working hours, the clickety-clack of hammers on stone—a sound I have never heard outside of the granite towns and which I will remember to my final day. There was the great strength and beauty of this stone; the cranes that lifted and carried it; the chips that were daily wheeled out to be added to the everlasting terminal moraines around the sheds; the smell of the slush, whatever it was, that was used to polish the granite.

Sometimes we boys would slip over to one of the stone-sheds on a day when nobody was working—Sunday, maybe. It was fascinating to wander among the half-worked stones, to inspect the tools abandoned when the closing whistle blew, to see the crane machinery all ready for work but still and unmanned. We never thought of a day when the tools would be laid down for the last time and the stationary engine and crane would work no more in that place, nor the men who operated them.

There were, I suppose, three worlds in Williamstown: the world of the stone-sheds, the world of the villagers, and the world of the farmers. We boys found mysteries in the worlds of the Italians and the French Canadians, but these worlds were not completely strange. Or they were no more strange than the worlds of all adults, for we boys were a community to ourselves.

As I look at a picture of the children of the Williamstown Graded School, taken about 1898, give or take a year, I can detect the Scotch and Welsh blood in boys or girls whose names I remember, one or two with French Canadian names, none that I am sure were Italian, although this doesn't mean there were none, and, of course, the Irish. There is one boy I have always thought looked like Huck Finn—he still does, in this photograph. There is one girl, I thought then and long afterwards, as beautiful as the dawn; I think I can see why I thought so, but I am not quite sure.

This picture was taken on the broad front steps of the school, with the teachers standing at the top. Some of them I remember, but not their names. How would I answer today should one of them ask me, as she did once, to bound Europe and Asia, naming each body of water, each bay, gulf, and strait, all the way round? I was able to do so then but now—though I would like to please her, for she has a pleasant face—I am not sure I could.

Where now is the Barents Sea? What became of it after 1917? What became of the small, ineffectual-looking boy who sits fourth from the left on the top steps in the picture? His ears stuck out like wings, but his hair was dark and plentiful.

I try to get back into this picture, and at times and for brief instants I can do so. My brother seems to have a hole in the knee of one of his long stockings; so have I. I believe these must have happened since we left home an hour or so ago, or that we managed to get out without our mother seeing us. Our mother always wanted us to look as well as we could; she was quick with the darning needle and she could tie a flowing bow, of the sort a small boy wore then, as neatly as any woman in town.

But I am not thinking so much of the passage of time as of the dwindling of a town. For though Williamstown did not break up, as Merrill Linton's father had been afraid it would, it did shrink. What was there in 1898, in that golden year, that could cast such a shadow?

As early as that year there appeared, at rare intervals, a Thing with wheels but no horse that nevertheless managed to move along our dusty, muddy, and rocky roads. This was a spectacle we wouldn't miss for anything, but we saw it as a free outdoor circus, not as a portent of the future.

We argued over what it should be called. Many persons said it was a horseless carriage—as, indeed, it was. Others called it an automobile and were rebuked by writers in the *Youth's Companion* and other publications, who said you could not unite a Greek root with a Latin root. This mattered to me, even at the age of ten, after I had heard my father and Mr. Ainsworth argue it.

But the Thing itself, whatever it was called, remained marvelous and incredible. It made a terrific noise. It was always breaking down. Yet it could go from Williamstown to Barre, if all went well, in not much over half an hour; and if it ran at all it could go when its owner wanted it to.

The Thing with wheels but no horse made buggy rides obsolete and, without meaning to, killed the Williamstown I knew.

The Thing killed Williamstown, and not out of cussedness but because it was so demanding. The Thing did not like dust or mud. The Thing had no thought of a road taken at leisure, tasted and relished; the Thing had to be somewhere at a given time, anyhow in a great hurry; the Thing wished to dash, not stroll.

I don't know what happened to J. K. Linton's store, except that after my time it became a farmers' co-operative, and after that, it burned down and was physically replaced by a filling station. If it hadn't been for the Thing there would, of course, have been no need for a filling station. When I was ten years old I didn't know what a filling station was. Nobody did. There were none.

It is just as easy to explain why the hotel went away as it is to explain why the J. K. Linton store—dissolved into ashes, the smoke of it rising into a clear sky full of images—went away. The hotel burned down. So did the stone-sheds. But a store, a hotel, a stone-shed, would grow again if the soil were fit for them. In 1898 it was fit for them. Later it wasn't.

The roads were measured by time, and time in 1898 went slowly. I would have needed an hour, at least, to get to Barre by horse-drawn buggy, and perhaps another hour and a half to get back, since getting back was uphill.

Therefore Williamstown could have, and had to have, a hotel, several stores, three churches, and, if business seemed good, two or three granite-cutting sheds. Williamstown was an island in time as time was measured in 1898, and an island must provide itself with the necessities of life.

Williamstown could do this, no matter what it took in from the outside world. It didn't make all its own flour, but it could have; nor process all its own meat, but it could have; nor raise all its own vegetables, but it could have; nor much of its own fruit, but yet it had apples enough, and berries, and a cherry or two; nor provide all its own lumber, but it came near doing this. Williamstown people could have stayed alive for a long while if the Central Vermont Railway had stopped running and the dirt roads had been blocked. Life would have been Spartan but not impossible.

How did Williamstown begin to wane from its high position? Was it dying, a little, in my time? What stabbed it harder—some quirk in the granite industry that shifted the movement of stone to Barre and Montpelier; or the weapon that struck at all the small towns from ocean to ocean, from border to border—the gasoline-driven Thing, the smooth highway, the consequent shrinking of the map, so that a market town every thirty miles, say, could take the place of a market town every ten miles or so?

I didn't see anything at all going on, during my time,

that suggested the great changes that were to come. A boy of ten wouldn't—boys of ten are almost never philosophers, economists, sociologists, or historians.

So there was Williamstown, and there was the year 1898. Our family began to disperse a little later, and that is too long a story for the present. I myself left Williamstown in 1901 to go to high school in Waterbury, Vermont, with kindly help from my aunt and maternal grandmother. That, too, is another story—there are so many other stories.

Since this is a guided tour of Williamstown as it seemed to a ten-year-old boy in the year 1898, I propose now to explore again, briefly and finally, this vanished dominion.

This is a high valley among the hills, where the Indians long ago raised corn. If I went uptown from the General E. Bass house, I had the lovely brick building of the Sibley farm on my left, with its attendant barns and the meadows stretching level for I suppose a quarter mile or so. On my right would be Mr. Ainsworth's meadows, not much used at that time except for producing hay. As I neared the Pool Bridge, where the brook crossed the road, I might see marshes on either hand if it were spring or early in a rainy fall. There was a modern house or maybe two such on the Sibley side and a stone wall on the Ainsworth side.

The Pool Bridge was overhung with willows. The nature of the stream underneath changed from year to year as the sand migrated upstream or downstream, I never knew why. Dace swam in it, and suckers lingered patiently for the baited hook, knowing perhaps that few cared to bother catching them but hoping to

be appreciated and compared with trout once they were in the frying pan.

The bridge had a sort of bulwark on each side, covered with corrugated iron and overhanging a little. I used to cross this bulwark on the outer side, hanging by my hands. Other boys weren't all courageous enough to do this, and after a while I wasn't either. Where did all that valor go, I wonder, when I needed it in later years?

After one crossed the bridge the village began. On the left there was a sort of tenement building, two stories high, with verandas, painted in a dark brown, gloomy in winter but pleasantly cool in summer.

Beyond, on the left, was the schoolhouse, a squared-off structure with no architectural pretensions whatever; and though in 1898 I welcomed vacations, I loved this school and most of the teachers who taught there.

On the right, almost opposite, lived Mr. and Mrs. Liberty Jeffords, a respected elderly couple to whom I sometimes spoke when Mrs. Jeffords consented to bake some loaves of bread for the Duffus family. These smelled so good I almost ate them up on my way home.

Farther along, and still on the right, was the Linton residence—a happy, comfortable place during J. K.'s good days. I remember it in brown paint, and I suspect it wasn't one of the oldest houses in the village. The last time I saw it, the paint was peeling badly, and my heart ached a little.

So, on my way upstreet, I came to many houses and other structures that had meaning for me. There was George Beckett's harness shop and his new house and the older house on the back of the lot where we lived for a while later on; there was the Edison Girls' brick

house on the left; there was in succession, on the left, the Town Hall, the Universalist Church, the Congregationalist Church, and the Methodist Church; there were, on the right, the stores, beginning with a modest establishment run by a Mr. Brockway, an elderly man with a short beard and a quiet disposition. I don't now see how Mr. Brockway made his living, and maybe he didn't; maybe he only thought he did. His stock was crowded higgledy-piggledy into a rather small, dark room; he had a pronounced lack of enthusiasm about everything; and though he was polite in a melancholy sort of way, I never saw many persons in his store, or heard the sort of conversation that was audible in J. K. Linton's establishment and that was so educational to young boys.

Beyond Mr. Brockway's store, still on the right, was the meat market where Ben Weaver would sell you a steak for twenty-five cents, but it would be a good steak, and maybe he would give a boy a slice of bologna free. He would also give away crackling, which was the residue from pork fat tried out to make lard; I didn't like this at all, but it was filling.

Then one came to the Linton store, the Monument House, the other drugstore—the one Fred Ainsworth didn't own—and the Seaver store, which I think sold clothes, furniture, and various odds and ends, and must have competed in some respects with J. K. Linton's establishment. And there were the three churches on the left.

By this time one would be about at the bridge, the upper bridge, with I forget what on the right side and the blacksmith shop on the left side. On the far side of the bridge a road led up to the box factory and then into farm country. I think there was a cheese factory, too, and perhaps at that time, or a little earlier, they had put the cheese in boxes and shipped it out.

On such a tour of our village I would avoid the road to Barre, which kept straight ahead, and swing right toward Mill Village. The sawmill and the gristmill might engage me for a few minutes, and then I would swing right some more, past a wood-working shop above the mill dam; and this was often worth looking into—and smelled better than any perfume, except possibly new-mown hay and some scents of cooking.

There were a few modest houses beside the stream, and these, I believe, belonged to French-Canadian "lumpers" who worked in the stone-sheds. I was a little afraid of the French-Canadians, I can't recall why. They were, in general, I now realize, the best-natured of men, and when they threatened to kill each other they never intended to do so. But I hurried by, if I was alone.

Opposite these houses there was a farm, owned by I don't know whom, and what I remember of it now is the way it looked one fall—maybe the fall of 1898—when the field nearest the road had been planted to corn and pumpkins. I stole an ear of corn, which was hard chewing, but what I remember is the beauty of the yellow pumpkins among the brown stalks.

Our tour would now bring us past the Rattlesnake Tavern and so around to the stone-sheds and over another little bridge whence one could look across the marsh and the meadow and see the General E. Bass house.

Then one came to the railway station, and maybe, even after all this walking, it was still bright morning and Old Man Webb was at the throttle ready to take the train down the grade to Barre, and Jim Kennealy, the conductor, was yelling "B-o-a-r-r-r-r-d!" the way an old-fashioned conductor always did, as though two or three thousand people were waiting for the word.

I did not, in fact, leave Williamstown until 1901. Yet now it seems to be time to step aboard. It is time, after this tour of 1898, to say goodbye to that year. Jim Kennealy repeats his "B-o-a-r-r-r-r-d!" Old Man Webb pulls his throttle and blows his whistle, and the fireman—ah, if only I could have been that fireman on at least one trip!—rings the bell frantically.

We are moving, gathering speed, down the grade to Barre and points north, south, east, and west. We are also headed toward the twentieth century. I look back with homesickness and forward with eagerness. Soon we are out of sight of Williamstown and the year 1898.

Daylight in the Swamp

CONTINUED FROM PAGE 12

nable. The timber line receded, and before long the lumberjacks began to notice signs in hotels and saloons that read "No Calked Boots Allowed Here." Civilization had caught up with them. As they peered forth from the middle of billions of stumps, the boys could see it was time to move again. There was always more timber west, just over the hump.

Perhaps a quarter of the migrating lumberjacks of the lake states moved into the southern pine region, but the main army moved west. A few stopped in Montana. More went on into Idaho. Still more of them crossed the Cascade Range and came down the Columbia, the Snohomish, and the Skagit, tossing from the windows of the steamcars the now-emptied bottles and snuffboxes they had bought in Duluth, in Chippewa Falls, in Muskegon, in Saginaw. They were cutting the Big Swath, the Big Clearing, and now, although they didn't know it, they were in their last stronghold. Their backs were to the mountains, their faces to the sea.

Here they were in the largest forests of big timber they had ever seen. There are two distinct forests. East of the Cascade Range the woods are dominated by the ponderosa pine (western yellow), standing up to 200 feet on the best sites and running to six feet in diameter. Between the Cascades and the sea is the Douglas fir, standing up to 325 feet, with diameters up to fifteen feet. In the fir region also are large stands of western red cedar of enormous girth; and in coastal strips called the rain forest are stands of Sitka spruce and west coast hemlock. (The latter, for many years rarely considered worth cutting, has come into its own with the rise of the pulp and paper industry.)

Along with the loggers, even if most historians have rather prudishly ignored it, came a notable migration of fancy women from the old sawdust towns. They had seen altogether too much daylight in the swamps of the lake states; and now the more enterprising among them went out and bought new bonnets with sweeping feathers and one-way tickets to Spokane or Portland or Seattle.

In Montana and Idaho and in eastern Oregon and Washington, the loggers continued to use horses, but west of the Cascades, it was found, the timber was much too big for such temperamental animals. What was needed here was a lot of power and a slow, steady pull, so the west-side loggers reverted to the primordial force of the eastern pineries—oxen—only here they were called bulls. Sleds would not do to handle the big sticks. There was seldom snow enough

for sledding anyway, and there were few streams deep and wide enough for good river driving. But the boys were adaptable—they invented the skid road.

The skid road was the western loggers' first and greatest contribution to the technology of the woods. A path was cleared in the forest. At suitable intervals trees were felled across the path, cut free of limbs, then half-buried in the soft ground. These were the skids that made a skid road, a sort of track to keep moving logs from hanging up on rocks or miring in mud.

It was crude, yet effective. They hitched the bulls to the logs—five or six, maybe ten yokes of them, in charge of the bullwhacker, or teamster, who was perhaps the all-time master of profanity, and the big sticks, held in tandem by hooks, were pulled over the skids. It was something to see, this skid-road logging. First, you heard the clank of chains and the loud, clear call of the bullwhacker's voice echoing down a forest road that was like a deep green canyon, so tall and thick stood the Douglas fir. Then the powerful line of red and black and spotted white would swing by with measured tread, the teamster, sacred goadstick over his shoulder, walking beside the team, petting and cursing them by turns. Back of the bulls walked the skid greaser, daubing thick oil on the skids, which smoked from friction. And then came the huge logs themselves, sliding along with a dignified roll.

Bull-team logging was drama. Small boys in Oregon and Washington, late in the last century, wanted to be bullwhackers when they grew up. More than a few authentic timber barons started to make their piles by whacking their own bulls down a skid road. Even the term "skid road" survives long after the last bull team has disappeared. In modern usage it refers to that district of western towns which, says the big Webster quite correctly, is "the part of a town frequented by loggers."

Use of the word in this sense originated seventy-odd years ago in Seattle, where Henry Yesler's pioneer skid road ran through the settlement from the timbered hills to the mill on tidewater. It was natural that hotels and saloons and other dives seeking logger trade should have been established along the skid road, and in good time the entire neighborhood became known as The Skidroad, a logical and useful term that quickly spread to all Far Western towns. Of recent years an abominable corruption has appeared, "skid row," whose use is confined to the glib who wish to appear sophisticated but patently don't know what they are talking about.

Bull-team technique developed one serious fault, best described by the maxim that any operator who attempted to haul logs more than one mile to a saw-mill, or to water where they could be floated, was heading straight for bankruptcy. What was more, that mile must be a downhill haul, or at least level. Such a limit could not last long in a country where operators could lift their eager eyes to see billions of feet of fine timber all over the foothills, the valleys, even the mountains up to, say, the 4,000-foot level.

It is the history of technology that it advances according to need; and it was an inventive logger, John Dolbeer of Humboldt Bay, California, who in 1881 devised the rig that was to drive the bull teams from the woods. Dolbeer's invention, which he patented in 1882, was a new kind of donkey engine with a single cylinder, a vertical boiler, and a horizontal engine with a drum, or capstan. Though other men were simultaneously experimenting with steam in the Douglas-fir forest, they left no clear record, and the Dolbeer became the machine that supplanted the ox. By the early nineties Dolbeers were operating in Oregon and Washington.

The Dolbeer brought ground-lead logging: By means of a cable pulled by the turning capstan, the logs were led along the ground to a "yard." Once a turn was in, a line horse hauled the cable back into the timber. The animals became very knowing, needing scarcely any guidance at all. A man listed on the payroll as "sniper" prepared the felled logs for easy yarding by rounding their head-ends with an axe. "Choker men" put wire slip loops called chokers around the logs, then hitched the chokers to the main line from the donkey engine. On a high stump stood the signal boy. When the yarding crew's boss yelled "Hi!" the boy dipped his flag, or waved an arm, and the engineer put on the steam.

Ground-lead logging brought speed and volume. Throughout the nineties and well into this century, the donkeys grew in size and power to meet the increased production of the mills. By the turn of the century the influx of eastern operators and their men was getting into full swing in the Northwest. Camps grew from an average of perhaps 20 to more than 200 men each. Railroads were being laid to haul the logs from camp to mill, or to tidewater.

Rail logging had been made feasible by perfection of a geared locomotive credited in large part to Ephraim Shay, a Michigan logger as bearded as Moses and something of a prophet himself. A Shay engine could negotiate grades and curves that would have defeated a rod locomotive. This was sufficient. Old Shay's name went honorably into logging history.

Then, one inspired day, some unidentified logger in a hurry figured out a method to improve the ground-lead system. What he did was to hang a block or pulley high up in a big tree. Thus was the high-lead born. Through the block ran the main line from the donkey engine. A log could now be yarded with its head end in the air, riding free above the stumps and underbrush. The line horse was supplanted by an extra drum on the donkey, the haulback, which returned the main line to the woods after each turn more quickly than a horse could turn around. The high-lead speeded production almost beyond knowing. It also brought into being the most spectacular occupation in the timber, or perhaps anywhere—that of the high-rigger or high-climber.

With sharp steel spurs on his legs, a safety belt around his waist, and an axe and saw dangling from a rope beneath, this steeple jack of the woods hitches himself up a tall fir, limbing as he goes. At somewhere around 150 feet from the ground he straps himself in place and saws off the treetop. Hanging there against the sky, he must work carefully lest he cut his belt and crash to his death on the circle of stumps below. When the great top starts to lean, then to fall, the high-climber must brace himself well. The trunk vibrates wickedly in wide arcs. For an instant, top and man are little more than a blur. Down goes the top, tons of it, to crash on the forest floor and send echoes up the canyon.

The topped trunk is now a spar tree—an anchor for subsequent high-lead operations. It is guyed all around with steel cables. Then the high-lead block, weighing some 1,800 pounds, is hoisted to the top and secured. The main line is run through the block and its end taken into the woods by the haulback. When a turn of logs has been hooked to the main line, the signal-boy, now called a "whistle-punk," gives the go-ahead. The huge donkey engine snorts noise and steam and sparks; then, rearing up like some prehistoric monster from the underbrush, comes an imposing sight—a log six feet in diameter, forty feet long. It is yanked swiftly, one end dragging, surging, the head end clear, to the donkey where it is unhooked by the "chaser," and the rigging sent flying back into the timber.

High-lead logging almost doubled production. It also brought a notable increase in the accident rate, which was already far too high. With timber sailing through the air, rather than moving with moderate speed over the ground, there was an infinitely greater chance for a man to be hit—and harder. Added to this natural hazard was the yarding bonus offered by many logging operators. The boss, the "bull of the woods," set a footage quota, usually high rather than otherwise, for the crew. If they managed to yard more than this figure, every man got a dollar or so added to his wages that day. It was the timber-country version of the industrial speed-up. If it doubled production, it also doubled accidents; and it may well have tripled discontent.

Discontent among the loggers did not originate in the Northwest. There had been strikes, chiefly against the twelve-hour day then in force, back in Michigan. There had been protests over low wages and poor working conditions in Wisconsin and Minnesota. Yet labor unions failed to get a real foothold. Only the shingle weavers of the Far West cedar mills had managed to keep alive an organization of any effectiveness, and it had nothing to do with loggers.

It was often said of loggers—and they believed it themselves—that their isolation and the nature of their work made them individualists unfit to band together against the boss. And the babel of tongues characteristic of logging camps from the eighties onward was no help. But now, in the first decade of the new century, came a new union, the Industrial Workers of the World, led by Big Bill Haywood, an ebullient, one-eyed hard-rock miner who had also worked in the woods. He had just become labor's hero in a sensational trial in Idaho in which he was acquitted of a murder charge. Advocating a dictatorship of the proletariat, the I. W. W., or "wobblies," as they were called, were shrewd enough to go after membership by promising loggers higher wages, better food, the eight-hour day, safe working conditions, and almost anything else which organizers could think up to bring the boys running to get the Little Red Card denoting I. W. W. membership.

The wobblies were less a labor union than a religion. They staged strikes, first in Portland, later in the Willapa and Grays Harbor logging camps, then in Seattle, Spokane, and Everett. When they couldn't pull a strike on the job, it was their delight to get themselves arrested for speaking on the streets; then they would shout that they were making a "free speech fight," meanwhile sending word out over the remarkable wobbly grapevine for the boys to rally in number. They came in number, too, commonly on freight trains, to fill town and city jails to overflowing and make bedlam for days and nights on end. Among their organizers was a woman, Elizabeth Gurley Flynn— young, handsome, a flaming red tie at her throat— possessed of enough eloquence to send skid-road males hurrying to get their membership cards in the nearest wobbly hall.

Though the I. W. W. never troubled to consolidate its gains in the manner of conventional unions, it did

put the fear of God, or possibly of Marx, into the lumber barons. Violence broke out sporadically in the camps and the sawmill centers—not just the violence of clubs and stones and brass knuckles but of guns in the hands of desperate and determined men who were playing for keeps.

Neither unions nor laws nor the slow national decline in the per capita consumption of lumber could put a stop to the steady progress of logging technology. Steam had inspired uncounted inventors to experiment with power machinery. In steep country, counterbalance incline railroads appeared. A primeval steam saw for felling timber, a forerunner of today's gas-driven chainsaw, was built and tried. A noted woods boss, C. C. (Whitewater) McLean, left his name secure in the industry by inventing the McLean load-

ing boom. Some genius around Puget Sound came up with a truly fearsome combination of steam, wheels, and lines he called a Walking Dudley. Other men were already playing with the idea of a tall yet portable steel mast to perform the duties of a spar tree. And at least two brave fellows rolled into the timber aboard a monstrous overland steam engine they hoped would replace both a yarding donkey and a locomotive. It didn't.

Then, on a day heavy with portent—unmarked in history, it may have been in 1911, or even 1913— somebody went into the woods with a homemade truck operated by an internal-combustion engine, loaded it with logs, and drove it away to the sawmill on a road made of planks laid end to end. Here was a warning of things to come. Steam was to be driven slowly yet relentlessly from the woods by gasoline and diesel oil. A great thundering era was ending.

But not yet. There were still 3,400 miles of standard-gauge logging tracks in Oregon and Washington—over half the total in seven western states and the province of British Columbia—in 1929, a peak year when almost twelve billion board feet of timber went to the sawmills of the two states, most of it by rail. It was hauled by more than 600 steam locomotives, of which 400 were geared engines made by Lima-Shay, Climax, and Heisler; the rest were engines from Baldwin, Porter, American, and Vulcan.

Back in the early 1920's, I used to know gray old loggers, shaggy-headed and grown dim of eye, who would sit on the deacon seat, of an evening in camp, and damn the "modern" methods, by which they meant steam logging, and weep for the days when noble bull teams lurched down the skid roads, bellowing and grunting, while the bullwhacker cried aloud in protest to a Deity who had made such miserable oxen. In *that* great time, it seemed, men had been men, with hair not only on their chests but on their faces too. My own generation, according to these veterans, was a group of sheared weaklings dependent on machinery, coddled in camp with company mattresses, even sheets; with *white* crockery, not tin plates on the cookhouse table; with pretty female waitresses; with shower baths and electric lights; with mail and newspapers daily, or almost daily.

I realized, of course, that all this was merely a lament of ancient men for their youth, a youth gone now into the mists where ghostly bull teams walked a rotted skid road. Thus it is with me, thirty years later, when memory gives me pause to reflect on how little has survived of that so-called modern era I knew only yesterday. That era did not come to an end with a bang. Eras seldom do. But the logging railroad and the steam donkey had, by 1955, virtually disappeared in the Oregon and Washington timber. A few Shays work in West Virginia, but in general this locomotive is now an antique, drowsing with cast-iron generals in a park—a park past which highway trucks loaded with logs streak at dizzying speeds.

It makes my generation men out of Genesis; we can remember, for instance, when western loggers used snuff, not cigarettes. We can recall when loggers would eat hay, if you sprinkled a little whiskey on it. Above all, we can remember when logging was done by single men who lived in logging camps at the end of a railroad through the woods. Today, even the camps are passing, and loggers are young married men who prefer to live with their families in communities on the highway, to drive to and from the logging works in their own cars.

There is, however, one change in the industry which no man, no matter how beset with nostalgia, can fail to welcome. It is this: Every logging outfit worthy of the name—at least in the Pacific Northwest—has on its payroll from one to one hundred graduates of accredited forestry schools. Thirty years ago, the few foresters seen in the logging woods were exotics who had no more standing than a botanist. Loggers referred to them as bug-chasers, as pismire superintendents. No longer. Industrial foresters today advise cutting practices to be followed and are responsible for the care and protection of company lands—from which one crop has been harvested and another crop from ten to fifty feet tall is growing.

Such lands used to bear the timber baron's mark of Cain when he was Public Enemy Number Two, if not Number One, his devastated acres strewn with debris, ready for burning again and again. Today these lands are tree farms, registered as such and expensively cherished. Timber is a crop. Forests are everlasting. Such is the theory now held by major loggers and lumbermen all over the country, and the theory has largely turned to practice.

Now that both logging camp and logging railroad are on their way to join the bull teams and the skid roads, I imagine that few of today's loggers, by now thoroughly and, I trust, happily domesticated, regret their passing. Yet, here and there may be an old-timer with a stubborn atavistic streak who, when the melancholy is upon him, will suddenly recall a dawn, back when the world was new, when all of us were young and handsome, when all phonographs played "Margie" and "Dardanella," and the wireless was not yet quite radio.

It was a magic time filled with dreams, even at the far end of a logging railroad in a logging camp, where the sun came over the mountain to slant in whirling mists, while the bull cook beat the daylights out of the camp gong, and two hundred single young men came stomping down the camp walk, their calks clicking rhythmically on the planks, heading for an incredible breakfast, then a thundering ride behind the rolling Shay to where the spar tree rose high above the round stuff lying among the stumps far below.

Such was my "modern" time. I thought then that it was a thumping great and wildly wonderful, if tragically heedless, era in the timber. Thirty years later I know it was.

Stewart H. Holbrook of Portland, Oregon, has written many articles and books dealing with the Pacific Northwest. His first book, Holy Old Mackinaw, A Natural History of the American Lumberjack, *published in 1938 by Macmillan, has gone through seventeen printings and, in 1956, was brought out in a new, enlarged edition.*

So you're going to America

A letter to a French friend

By D. W. BROGAN

My Dear X,

I am delighted that you have made the plunge and decided to go to America. . . . But feeling, like all good Europeans, that the Americans owe us a living, as medieval monks and renaissance scholars felt that robber barons and *condottieri* owed them a living, I yet hope that you can get more out of this trip than a holiday, a few gadgets like electric razors and can openers, and the chance to see some of the French pictures that the Americans, in the past generation, have stolen with their ill-gotten dollars.

It is a conviction of mine (rare among European intellectuals) that there is more to be got from an American visit than that; that all of us, French, British, Italians, Germans, have something to learn, if only about ourselves, from a visit to the country that, like it or not, influences us, if only by breeding a crippling nausea and hatred, to a degree inconceivable as late as 1914. It is easy enough to insist on one thing you can do in going to America. No matter how much you hate and despise the country, no matter how much you resent its invasion of the old and civilized world, you owe it to your own intellectual dignity to try to understand how, when, why its shadow fell over us, *its* shadow, not that of the U.S.S.R., nor of the Third Reich, nor of the Rome-Berlin-Tokio axis. We may proudly boast that we are the architects of our own ruin, that by our own folly we precipitated the disaster of 1914-45; we may display the pride of the boy cycling up to and over the edge of a precipice, proudly announcing "Look! No hands"; but we have still to explain to ourselves why it was the *Americans* who picked us up and set us on our wobbly feet again. It is hard for all of us, or nearly all of us, to do this. It is especially hard for Frenchmen. Often enough and rightly, the French have cast themselves

as the Greeks (more accurately, as the Athenians) of the modern world, and the Athenians found it hard to take their Roman masters seriously. Read (this is a counsel I give my own snooty countrymen), read the first chapter of Polybius and see that sagacious Greek (but not Athenian) trying to persuade his fellow Hellenes that the fortune of the Roman state was a subject worthy of serious attention, not of snobbish peevishness or of irony and the Athenian equivalent of the wisecrack. Consider the Romans, ponderous, slow-witted, semi-savage (look at their games), ugly (look at their portrait busts), touching nothing that they did not deform (look at Venus as a version of Aphrodite), building, when they began to build, for size, like the Colosseum (the very name gives the thing away), or dull copies of the works of their betters, like the Maison Carrée. Why, generations of Greeks asked themselves, why should we do anything but mock them, flatter them, fleece them? Of course, they were right. The Romans had nothing to offer but riches, power, order, know-how, good drains (how Athens must have stunk!), and subsidies for deserving sophists.

It is hard, then, for a European intellectual, especially for a French intellectual, to approach the United States with any degree of objectivity. It is big, remote, mighty, probably boring. It will certainly be found boring if the visitor comes to it looking only for what will remind him of home. If anything does, it will make him either homesick or scornful. I can well understand a Frenchman feeling that the great French pictures in the American art galleries are sorrowful exiles. They—and he—ought to be elsewhere, in Provence or the Ile-de-France. They are as out of place as the Elgin marbles in the British Museum, in the gray air of London, the Egyptian and Assyrian antiquities in the Louvre, in the nearly as gray air of Paris. Avoid the American who wants you to admire something in America because it will remind you of something in Europe. "Boston is so like London" (it isn't)—"New Orleans is so like Marseille" (it isn't). Avert your eyes from the bogus Italian gardens and fountains you can find in Washington, from the châteaux of the Loire that you can find on the Illinois prairie or the *"cité"* of Carcassonne you can find in Maine. Avoid them as you would the Duomo of Milan or the Madeleine, or take them as seriously as they deserve, as monuments of bad or of irrelevant good taste.

What you must want to see are the American things. I won't waste time in recommending to you the unique natural sights—Niagara, the Grand Canyon, the Golden Gate. You can admire these safely; the Americans own them but didn't make them, possibly don't deserve them, any more than the Swiss deserve the Jungfrau. But what is harder to do is to accept the fact that there are novel American sights that the Americans have largely made and which you must, to some degree, understand and appreciate if you are not to be constantly bored or irritated. It will be difficult to do this if you arrive looking for European equivalents. You will be as deceived as the complacent French tourists in Italy whom Stendhal continually sneered at. You must be ready to admire the American achievement where it is admirable—and it will be most strange where it is most admirable.

I will not pretend—you would not believe me if I did—that I get anything like the same pleasure at seeing a silo arise over the horizon of the great fertile plain of Iowa that I get from seeing Chartres arising over the great fertile plain of the Beauce. With all due respect to Mr. Edmund Wilson, you can exaggerate the merits of plumbing, even of American plumbing. For one thing, it tends to lack variety. But the equivalent of Chartres is not the silo or the American county seat, provided, in most cases known to me, with the most outrageously ugly ecclesiastical buildings built by man's hands. It is the great bridges, dams, roadways and skyways; even, in a few cases, airports and railroad stations. You must, that is to say, go prepared to appreciate the equivalents of the Pont-du-Gard, not of the Parthenon. Maybe you are not prepared to do this. Maybe you are not prepared to give to New York the kind of admiration that Rome, Alexandria, Persepolis, possibly Carthage, got and deserved in the ancient world, that Haussmann's Paris got from Mark Twain, that great modern French achievements like the dams at Donzère-Mondragon or the Port of Dakar deserve and get from intelligent Americans. If nothing but the Parthenon or the Sainte-Chapelle will do, you will miss that kind of esthetic experience in America.

You will be worse off, not better off, if you come to America informed only by the current American authors most

admired by the mandarins of French taste. At one time in Paris, in the past few months, the French theatre-goer could see *Requiem for a Nun, God's Little Acre, Tea and Sympathy, Cat on a Hot Tin Roof, The Crucible.* A wide but still not representative range of the American theatre and American life! Literature is only to a limited degree a trustworthy picture of a country, and the literature of one country, as assessed and utilized in another, is a very treacherous guide indeed. The mistakes are inevitable; there are an inside and an outside view of a culture and to base one's view on those elements in a foreign literature that appeal most easily to foreign taste is dangerous indeed. *Clochemerle, Bonjour Tristesse, Les Mandarins*—are these American favorites an adequate sample of French literature today or an adequate guide to French life? In the French choice of the American authors to be admired and used as clues is not there some *parti pris*? Is there not some desire to be told that American life is deeply unhappy in an especially American way, that the boosting of the "American way of life" is a kind of whistling in the dark? And the American way of life seen in French fiction, in *La P. . . . Respectueuse,* in *Les Mandarins*? M. Sartre and Madame de Beauvoir are brilliant people. They can study, report on, assess remote, strange, rapidly changing, semi-secret societies with a confidence and speed that astonish me. Perhaps every Frenchman or Frenchwoman (especially if he or she is a philosopher), is what actors call a "quick study." I can only say that I, who have spent so much more time in the United States (and France) than either of them has in the U.S.A. or U.S.S.R., know what I know about those countries so much less clearly, decisively, and confidently than they know Russia, China, the United States, that I am full of admiration, in all senses of the term. Of course, one wonders what demon drove M. Sartre to censure his own vision in *Les Mains Sales*—and so to diminish the weight of his protest against the murder of freedom and truth in Hungary. One wonders (it is a less serious matter, but one wonders all the same) how much one can trust Madame de Beauvoir's vision of America when one notices that the Finno-American hero of *Les Mandarins* is given the very un-Finnish name of Brogan.

I suggest then that it would be a good idea for you to read

little or no French stuff on America, or to accept the possibility that it may not be quite right, to accept the possibility that more happens in the Deep South than Mr. Faulkner reports, as more happens in Bordeaux than M. Mauriac reports. No country investigates, reports, dissects itself with the candour and thoroughness of America. You need never go short of sound and illuminating reading matter! . . .

But Polybius or even Stendhal were not concerned merely to call the attention of their superior and snobbish countrymen to sights; they were concerned with social and political achievements, with what is called "a way of life." This phrase has been so much battered by vulgar propaganda, so much identified by silly Americans—and silly Europeans—with refrigeration, modern plumbing, Coca-Cola, the comics, highly unintellectual religion, a naïve optimism, that one is ashamed to use it. But it has to be used. After all, Pericles in the most famous speech of Greek antiquity was describing the Athenian way of life, in a speech that might have been used by the "Voice of Athens" had it been in existence. Virgil, underlining the arts in which the Roman should excel, was doing the same job as Pericles—and as Lincoln at Gettysburg, in the only funeral oration fit to be compared with that spoken by Pericles over the Athenian dead. "The American way of life" is not a simple matter of democracy or of gadgets and gimmicks, any more than the Athenian way of life was a simple matter of "freedom" or the Roman of law. And you will miss a great deal if you start out convinced that you *know* what it is and do not take trouble enough to modify—or perhaps reconstruct—your view of it.

Thus it may seem a platitude to repeat that the United States is very large and very varied, but it is a platitude so much and so easily forgotten that there can be no great sin in repeating it. The visitor to America, even if he is no novice in American matters, is always astonished, trapped, by the mere size of the United States. It seems to him extraordinary that so vast, so varied an area should be one country, one nation, one culture. It is, of course, better to be astonished than to fail to notice this highly relevant fact; it is better still to have some idea of the causes and the consequences of the apparent unity, and it is better still to note the limitations of the unity, the survival of the differences.

It *is* strange that so vast an area should be so unified that the superficial observer, especially if he travels by air, has so few of the normal ways of determining where he is. One city is very like another. . . . This uniformity that may well seem a deformity is yet a necessity and a political triumph. The uniformity and banality of much of American life, the pressure for conformity that has been feared and lamented since the time of Tocqueville is, as M. Raymond Aron has recently pointed out, the price of a unity maintained without the governmental coercion that holds the centrifugal forces of the Soviet Union in submission to the central power. There is probably no way in which this unity can be preserved without some degree of physical or moral coercion. Every political good has its price and we, in Europe, have certainly paid highly (and made the rest of the world pay highly) for our ferocious pursuit of national differentiation. The Americans have paid the same price—once; and the memory of their civil war, so living just below the surface,

accounts for that dislike of the doctrinal position pushed to its logical conclusion, to the complete autonomy of the individual or the region, which makes American politics so unsymmetrical and so irritating to Frenchmen, ready as they have been, and are, to sacrifice so much (of themselves and others) to the one, true, worthy, historically justified doctrine. The Americans tend to think that no political view of life is as certain, as important, as rightly demanding of sacrifice as all that. They are truer disciples of Montaigne than the countrymen of Montaigne.

The American Constitution is brief, elegant, ambiguous, in many ways mysterious. It is very unlike the Constitution that its framers planned; it is highly unlikely that the dominant interpretation of that Constitution, fifty years hence, will be that held by any American political school today. American unity is not a simple, coherent, easily defined, and limited idea; the Constitution is not a simple means of living happily ever after. Institutions of that simple kind are left to the more old-fashioned and romantic novelists. For them marriage is as definable a means to happiness as a political doctrine is to a Frenchman. For the Frenchman who would not, for a moment, think of taking seriously so simple a view of life in a novel will often accept it in a political programme. And the American who may be ready to read a nice, simple story, a "western" if he is a man, a "love story" if the American is a woman, rarely expects these elegant and happy solutions in political life. That things are not what they seem, that persons and problems change, while preserving the same names, that we create the world of illusions in which we live and love, these are truths about the human situation that the political American does not need to be told. He feels them. The Constitution has undergone as many changes—if you like, as many degradations—as a character in Proust. It is to themes like these that the American devotes his mind and his passions, and one possible price is an obvious simplicity in literature and philosophy. . . .

You will meet a good many "mandarins" or eggheads, and they will want to weep on your shoulder, lament the barrenness of American culture, the poorness of the bookshops, the horrors of soap opera. Don't take them too literally. They want sympathy, admiration, the assurance that they are defending the last citadels of culture. Some of the air-conditioned ivory towers you will visit are inhabited by people with persecution mania; some have suffered as much as if they had been French academics telling the truth about Algeria. Others have to have a bad-luck story, like a slightly passée woman lamenting her safely dead loves. Some have been really roughly treated. Some have to live in uncongenial surroundings, to meet on equal terms the professor of Butchering Practice, are forced to *coax* a board of business-minded trustees to buy a collection of Rimbaud letters or subsidize an *avant-garde* magazine. But don't spend too many tears on them. They will all turn up in Paris anyway.

Then reflect that many of the sorest eggheads you meet are lamenting a not very remote past when the professors *had* a lot of power (more than they have ever had in France). Many of them had what we call in England "a good war." They regret it, as so many of their French opposite numbers

83

regret the Resistance and the first heady years of the Liberation. "The contagion of the world's slow stain" is visible in Chicago and in Paris, the nostalgia for the "kingdom, the power and the glory."

But the average American has no such nostalgia, any more than the average Frenchman has. This is a lot better than the war years, than the Occupation or Iwo Jima.

There are differences, of course, basic differences between the most tragic American group experiences and the horrors of 1940-41. One reason why you may feel at home in the South is that the South had its occupation, its defeat, its intolerable sense of deception. But remember, even in the South, there was no shame like that of 1940, no scalawags like Pierre Laval.
. . . The American experience has been a much happier one (even in the South, even for the Negroes, in modern times) than the French (or German or Polish) experience. You are going to a country which has never known a famine, which has never known successful invasion from a totally foreign army, which has never really had to speculate on its survival. You are going to a country where it is necessary to add to the general sense of frustration that we have as humans to be adequately sad. Let American women tell you about American men and vice versa!

But you are in a country where friendliness, trust, a general social ease are in the air. It may not go very deep. Perhaps you can have very deep friendships only in a country where friendship is not lavished on everybody, where total strangers don't greet you with a cheerful but meaningless "hello." But people will be kind, open-handed, even, up to a point, open-hearted, to a degree that may fill you with suspicion. Put it aside for a moment; you will go far less wrong by taking this friendship at its face value than by assessing it.

You must remember that you are going to a country where the family, in the old, strong, if now declining French sense, does not exist, where nomadism is in the national blood, where traditions are adopted and discarded like the latest inspirations of the *haute couture,* where a great many serious things are discussed in what is a seriously shallow way, where people think that all problems have answers. (We, alas! know better. We are wiser, but also we ignore some solutions.)

You are going to a country where the relations between the sexes are complicated by the fiction that the American woman is boss of her docile man, who, in fact, is often only giving her a part of his mind; "too much poor quality attention." As a visitor you will be dealing with women in a society that promises them more than it gives (the opposite of

the English case, where so much more is given than promised). You are going to a country which tries everything once, where the most pompous businessman may have his "violin d'Ingres." (It may be the violin, the clarinet, painting, linguistics; you won't know at first and may never learn.) You are going to a country which does care a lot about children, which pampers them, which produces them on a scale beyond all Indian nightmares, which accepts an early exploitation of sexuality in a way that would shock a Paris industrial suburb (where is the Puritanism?), which believes in marriage, even repeated marriage, more than in love. You are going to a country where, suddenly, you can buy paper-back editions of everything, from Einstein to the Marquis de Sade, where more money is spent on music than on baseball and too much money, time, and energy are spent on golf, as the court of Louis XIV spent too much time, money, energy on hunting.

You are going to a country that has never known feudalism, has had no basic church and state quarrel, whose history is not cut in two by blood and massacre and treason. You are going to a country where fraternity is a permanent and often successfully attained social ideal, where liberty is never quite down and out, where equality is more of a reality than it is either in France or in England. (In all states outside the South and in some states inside the South, the son of a Negro worker or farmer has a better chance of obtaining a higher education than the son of a French worker has.)

You are going—but your attention has wandered. No matter, when you come back, you can talk to me of what you have seen, heard, read. You may still detest America; *tout comprendre est tout pardonner* is a silly saying, anyway. But just as a man deeply in love will prefer to have his *bien aimée* abused than ignored, I shall listen even to your abuse with interest, even with profit, *if* you have acted on my premise, if you have gone to America ready to accept the possibility that a new world has developed a new society, if you have imitated Polybius and not M. Jean-Paul Sartre.

Denis William Brogan, professor of political science at Cambridge University, England, has spent much time in the United States and has written often about America and her people. About this article, which appeared originally in The Virginia Quarterly Review, *Mr. Brogan writes: "The 'French friend' is notional; he is any European intellectual, formally hostile to the United States as an enemy of culture, a bearer of barbarism, et cetera." The drawings are by Gerry Gersten.*

"I'll Put a Girdle Round the Earth . . ." CONTINUED FROM PAGE 44

about five-eighths of an inch in thickness and weighed one ton per mile. This at once raised a serious problem, for the length needed to span the Atlantic weighed 2,500 tons—far too great a load to be carried in any single ship of the time.

The total cost of the cable was £224,000—at least £1,000,000 by today's standards, though it is about as difficult to relate our present currency to the Victorian pound's real purchasing power as to that of the Russian ruble.

The cable was completed within the remarkably short time of six months, and by July, 1857, it was ready to go to sea. By rights, Whitehouse should have sailed with it, but at the last moment he pleaded ill-health and Thomson was asked to fill the breach. It says much for the scientist's greatness of character that he agreed to do this, without any payment. This misshapen infant dumped on his doorstep was certainly not his baby, but he would give it the best start in life he could.

To share the enormous weight of the cable between them, the warships *Niagara* and *Agamemnon* had been provided by the United States and British governments respectively. The *Niagara* was the finest ship in the American Navy; the largest steam frigate in the world, she had lines like a yacht and her single screw could drive her with ease at twelve miles an hour. The *Agamemnon,* on the other hand, would not have looked out of place at Trafalgar; she was one of the last of the wooden walls of England, and though she had steam power as well as sail, one would not have guessed it by looking at her.

Both ships had been extensively modified to allow them to carry and pay out their 1,250 tons of cable. Their holds had been enlarged into circular wells or tanks in which the cable could be coiled; even so the *Agamemnon* was forced to carry several hundred tons of it on deck—a fact which later brought her to the edge of disaster.

After loading their respective halves of the cable, the two warships (with their escorts, the *Susquehanna* and the *Leopard*) sailed to their rendezvous at Valentia Bay, County Kerry. The plan that had been adopted, at the insistence of the directors, was for the *Niagara* to lay the whole of her cable westward from Ireland and for the *Agamemnon* to splice on in mid-Atlantic and then complete the job. This would have the advantage that the expedition would be in continual contact with land and could report progress

through the unwinding cable all the way across the Atlantic. On the other hand, if the ships arrived in mid-ocean during bad weather, and it was impossible to make the splice, half the cable would be lost.

The cable-laying began on Thursday, August 6, 1857. Almost at once there was a minor but annoying setback: five miles out, the cable caught in the primitive paying-out mechanism and broke. It was necessary to go back to the beginning, lift the section that had already been laid, and run along it until the break was reached.

"At length," Cyrus Field's brother Henry wrote, in his history of the cable-laying, "the end was lifted out of the water and spliced to the gigantic coil (i.e., the 1,250 miles in the *Niagara*'s hold) and as it dipped safely to the bottom of the sea, the mighty ship began to stir. At first she moved very slowly, not more than two miles an hour, to avoid the danger of accident; but the feeling that they are away at last is itself a relief. The ships are all in sight, and so near that they can hear each other's bells. The *Niagara,* as if knowing that she is bound for the land out of whose forests she came, bends her head to the waves, as her prow is turned towards her native shores."

All went well for the next three days, as reported in the London *Times:*

The cable was paid out at a speed a little faster than the ship, to allow for any inequalities at the bottom of the sea. While it was thus going overboard, communication was kept up constantly with the land. Every moment the current was passing between ship and shore. . . . On Monday they were over 200 miles to sea. They had got far beyond the shallow waters of the coast. They had passed over the submarine mountain . . . where Mr. Bright's log gives a descent from 550 to 1750 fathoms within eight miles. Then they came to the deeper waters of the Atlantic, where the cable sank to the awful depth of two thousand fathoms. Still the iron cord buried itself in the waves, and every instant the flash of light in the darkened telegraph room told of the passage of the electric current. . . .

But not for much longer—for at nine o'clock that morning the line suddenly went dead. There was a gloomy consultation among the engineers and all hope had been abandoned when, quite unexpectedly, signals started coming through again. This two and a half hour break in continuity was never satisfactorily explained; it might have been due to a faulty connection in the equipment at either end, or to a flaw in the cable itself.

This was a disturbing setback, but the next day

A Harper's Weekly *comment on the temporarily successful cable of 1858.*

brought catastrophe. The cable had been running out so rapidly (at six miles an hour against the ship's four) that it was necessary to tighten the brake on the paying-out mechanism. By an unfortunate error, the tension was applied too suddenly, and the cable snapped under the strain.

There was nothing to do but to postpone the attempt until the next year, since the amount of cable in the tanks was not sufficient to risk another try. But Field and his colleagues, though disappointed, were not despondent. They had successfully laid 335 miles of cable, a third of it in water more than two miles deep, and had been in telegraphic communication with land until the moment the line had parted. This proved, it seemed to them, that there was nothing impossible in the job they were attempting.

[The *Niagara* and the *Agamemnon* returned to England and deposited the remaining 2,200 miles of cable at Plymouth. After Field returned to the United States, he somehow succeeded, despite the fact that the Panic of 1857 was in full swing, in raising enough American

and British capital for the next year's effort. He used some of it to order 700 additional miles of cable. Meanwhile, two technical improvements were made. To prevent a repetition of the cable-snapping, a new paying-out mechanism was designed, with a brake that would automatically release if too much tension were applied. And in his laboratory at Glasgow University Professor Thomson developed his famous mirror galvanometer, a much more sensitive signal detector which would enable messages to be sent over the cable much more quickly once it was successfully laid.]

In the spring of 1858, the great enterprise got under way again. Once more the *Agamemnon* and the *Niagara* were commissioned as cable-layers and the Admiralty provided the sloop *Gorgon* as an escort. At Field's urging, the British Navy also loaned him the *Valorous* as a replacement for the U.S.S. *Susquehanna*, quarantined in the West Indies with yellow fever aboard.

This time, at the insistence of the engineers, it was

decided to start from mid-Atlantic and let the ships lay the cable in opposite directions. Not only would this be more economical in time, but it would mean that the all-important splice could be made at leisure, when weather conditions were most suitable.

After some initial tests in the Bay of Biscay (where, almost a hundred years later, the components of the Atlantic telephone cable also had their baptism of deep water), the little fleet sailed from Plymouth under fair skies on June 10, 1858. Once again Whitehouse had asked to be excused on medical grounds, and once again Thomson took his place—unpaid. It was lucky for Whitehouse that he stayed on land, for only two days after they had left harbor beneath clear skies, the four ships ran into one of the worst Atlantic storms ever recorded.

They were scattered over the face of the sea, each ship fighting desperately for its life. The *Agamemnon* was in particular danger, made almost unmanageable by the 1,300 tons of cable in her hold and by the more serious hazard of 250 tons coiled on deck. As Nicholas Woods reported in the London *Times:*

But all things have an end, and this long gale—of over a week's duration—at last blew itself out, and the weary ocean rocked itself to rest. . . . As we approached the place of meeting the angry sea went down. The *Valorous* hove in sight at noon; in the afternoon the *Niagara* came in from the north; and at even, the *Gorgon* from the south; and then, almost for the first time since starting, the squadron was reunited near the spot where the great work was to have commenced fifteen days previously—as tranquil in the middle of the Atlantic as if in Plymouth Sound.

After this ordeal, one would have thought the expedition had earned the right to success. The battered vessels were made shipshape, the cable ends were spliced together, and on June 26 the *Niagara* sailed west for Newfoundland and the *Agamemnon* headed east toward Ireland.

They had gone only three miles when the cable fouled the paying-out machinery on board the *Niagara* and snapped. This was anticlimax number one, but nobody was too upset, since little time and cable had been lost.

On the second attempt the ships got eighty miles apart before anything went wrong. Then they suddenly lost telegraphic contact, and each assumed that the cable had broken aboard the other. They hurried back to the rendezvous and hailed each other simultaneously with the words, "How did the cable part?" It was very disconcerting to find no explanation for what had happened; for some unknown reason, the cable had broken on the sea bed.

A third time the splice was made and, no doubt with all aboard wondering when they would meet again, the ships sailed apart once more. Unfortunately, it was not a case of third time lucky. After 200 miles had been paid out, the cable parted on the *Agamemnon*. The ships were now short of provisions, and according to prearranged plans they headed back independently to Ireland for a council of war.

It was an unhappy board of directors that met to consider the next move. Some, in despair, wished to sell the remaining cable and abandon the whole enterprise. But Field and Thomson argued for a fresh attempt, and in the end their counsel prevailed. The faint-hearted directors resigned in disgust at such stubborn foolishness, but by July 29 the ships were back in mid-Atlantic, ready for the fourth try.

There was no ceremony or enthusiasm this time when the splice went overboard and the ships parted. Many felt that they were on a fool's errand; as Field's brother remarked in his memoirs, "All hoped for success, no-one dared to expect it."

And certainly no one could have guessed that they were about to achieve, in the highest degree, both success and failure.

It was just as well for the American press that it had no representative on board the *Niagara,* for the westward voyage was a monotonously peaceful one, with the cable paying out uneventfully hour after hour. The only excitement was in the electricians' cabin, for twice during the week the signals from the *Agamemnon* failed but came back again in full strength after a few hours' anxiety. Apart from this, the *Niagara*'s log records "light breeze and moderate sea" almost all the way, until the moment she arrived in Trinity Bay, Newfoundland, with her 1,030 miles of cable safely strung across the bed of the Atlantic.

The eastward-sailing *Agamemnon*, on the other hand, had once again had an adventurous voyage, and several times had skirted mechanical or electrical disaster. Considering the conditions under which Thomson and his assistants worked, it is astonishing that they were able to keep their instruments operating at all. Listen to this description of the telegraph room as given by the Sydney *Morning Herald:*

The electrical room is on the starboard side of the main deck forward. The arrangements have been altered several times in order to avoid the water which showers down from the upper deck. At one end of the little place the batteries are ranged on shelves and railed in. . . . The most valuable observation is taken in sending on the marine galvanometer. Three seconds before it is taken, the clerk who times all the observations by a watch regulated by a chronometer too valuable to be brought into so wet a place says, "Look out." The other clerk at once fixes his eye on the spot of light, and immediately the word is given "Now" records the indication. This testing is made from minute to minute, so that a flaw is detected the moment it occurs.

The ships had spliced the cable on July 29, 1858, midway between Europe and America, in water 1,500 fathoms deep. To let the *Times* continue the story:

For the first three hours the ships proceeded very slowly, paying out a great quantity of slack, but after the expiration of this time, the speed of the *Agamemnon* was increased to about five knots, the cable going at about six. . . . Shortly after 6 o'clock a very large whale was seen approaching the starboard bow at a great speed, rolling and tossing the sea into foam all around. . . . It appeared as if it were making direct for the cable, and great was the relief of all when the ponderous living mass was seen slowly to pass astern, just grazing the cable where it entered the water. . . .

A few hours later there was a real crisis, vividly depicted by the Sydney *Morning Herald*'s reporter:

We had signalled the *Niagara* "40 miles submerged" and she was just beginning her acknowledgement when suddenly, at 10 p.m., communication ceased. According to orders, those on duty sent at once for Dr. Thomson. He came in a fearful state of excitement. The very thought of disaster seemed to overpower him. His hand shook so much that he could scarcely adjust his eyeglass. The veins on his forehead were swollen. His face was deathly pale. After consulting his marine galvanometer, he said the conducting wire was broken, but still insulated from the water. . . . There did not seem to be any room for hope; but still it was determined to keep the cable going out, that all opportunity

Harper's Weekly, MAY 2, 1857

A sketch, actual size, of the 1857 cable. Its copper conductor was protected by gutta-percha, hemp, and iron wire.

might be given for resuscitation. The scene in and about the electrical room was such as I shall never forget. The two clerks on duty, watching with the common anxiety depicted on their faces, for a propitious signal; Dr. Thomson, in a perfect fever of nervous excitement, shaking like an aspen leaf, yet in mind keen and collected, testing and waiting. . . . Mr. Bright, standing like a boy caught in a fault, his lips and cheeks smeared with tar, biting his nails and looking to the Professor for advice. . . . The eyes of all were directed on the instruments, watching for the slightest quiver indicative of life. Such a scene was never witnessed save by the bedside of the dying. . . . Dr. Thomson and the others left the room, convinced that they were once more doomed to disappointment. . . .

But they were not. No one ever knew exactly what

had happened; perhaps the cable's conducting core had broken under the strain of laying, but reunited on the sea bed when the tension was relaxed, and the elasticity of the coverings brought the wires together again. In any event, the signals returned at last, and the cable spoke again.

Our joy was so deep and earnest that it did not suffer us to speak for some seconds. But when the first stun of surprise and pleasure passed, each one began trying to express his feelings in some way more or less energetic. Dr. Thomson laughed right loud and heartily. Never was more anxiety compressed into such a space. It lasted exactly one hour and a half, but it did not seem to us a third of that time. . . .

The ship now began to run into heavy seas and started to pitch and roll in a manner that put a great strain on the cable.

During Sunday the sea and wind increased, and before the evening it blew a smart gale. Now indeed were the energy and activity of all engaged in the operation tasked to the utmost . . . the engineers durst not let their attention be removed from their occupation for one moment, for on their releasing the brake on the paying-out gear every time the stern of the ship fell into the trough of the sea entirely depended the safety of the cable. . . . Throughout the night, there were few who had the least expectation of the cable holding on till morning, and many remained awake listening for the sound that all most dreaded to hear—namely, the gun which should announce the failure of all our hopes. But still the cable, which, in comparison with the ship from which it was paid out, and the gigantic waves among which it was delivered, was but a mere thread, continued to hold on, only leaving a silvery phosphorus line upon the stupendous seas as they rolled on towards the ship. . . .

Quite apart from the extreme danger to the cable, the need to maintain speed caused the supply of coal to dwindle at an alarming rate. At one time it looked as if it would be necessary to start burning up the spars and planking in a grand finale like the last lap of *Around the World in 80 Days*. But luckily the gale slowly abated; both the *Agamemnon* and her cable had weathered the storm.

There was a brief flurry of excitement toward the end of the voyage when an inquisitive American barque bore down upon the telegraph fleet as it plowed along on its predetermined and unalterable course. The escorting *Valorous* had to fire her guns to scare away the interloper, who was doubtless surprised by such a rude reception. Luckily, no international incident resulted from this display of arms, though as the *Times* put it: "Whether those on board her considered that we were engaged in some filibustering expedition, or regarded our proceedings as another British outrage against the American flag, it was impossible to say; but in great trepidation she remained hove-to until we lost sight of her."

But at last, on the morning of Thursday, August 5:

the bold and rocky mountains which entirely surround the wild and picturesque neighborhood of Valentia, rose right before us at a few miles distance. . . . Soon after our arrival, a signal was received from the *Niagara* that they were preparing to land, having paid out one thousand and thirty nautical miles of cable, while the *Agamemnon* had accomplished her portion of the distance with an expenditure of one thousand and twenty miles, making the total length of the wire submerged two thousand and fifty geographical miles.*

Europe and America had at last been linked together. The news of this completely unexpected success, when all but a few enthusiasts had been convinced that the enterprise was hopeless, created a sensation. To read the papers of the time, one would think that the millennium had arrived. Even the staid *Times,* not prone to hyperbole, informed its readers: "The Atlantic is dried up, and we become in reality as well as in wish one country. . . . The Atlantic Telegraph has half undone the Declaration of 1775, [sic] and has gone far to make us once again, in spite of ourselves, one people. . . ."

There were, of course, celebrations all over the United States; countless sermons were preached, many of them based on the Psalmist's verse: "Their line is gone out through all the earth, and their words to the end of the world."

When a message from Queen Victoria to President Buchanan was received on August 16, further rejoicings and demonstrations broke out, to such effect that the roof of the New York City Hall was ignited by fireworks and the whole structure barely saved from the flames. In England, Charles Bright received a knighthood at the early age of 26 for his work as chief engineer of the project; in New York, on September 1, Cyrus Field was given a vast public ovation—at the very moment, ironically enough, when the Atlantic telegraph had given up the ghost.

For the cable that had been laid with such expense and difficulty, and after so many failures, was slowly dying. Indeed, when one considers the imperfections in its manufacture, and the various ordeals it had gone through, it is astonishing that it had ever worked at all.

* This is an error; the reporter had forgotten that the nautical mile is 15 per cent longer than the geographical mile, so that the total length of cable laid was about 2,350 miles. The actual great-circle distance between the two ends of the cable was 1,950 miles, the difference being due to the slack or excess cable which had to be laid to follow the contours of the sea bed.

Samuel F. B. Morse helped prove the feasibility of long-distance submarine telegraphy, but resigned as Field's electrician when he was maneuvered off the company's board.

In his effort to prove that no direct Atlantic line could be an economic proposition, a Colonel Tal Shaffner was later to produce a full transcript of the 1858 cable's working. It is a record of defeat and frustration—a four-week history of fading hopes. Even after five days had been allowed for setting up the receiving and transmitting equipment, this log of *all* the messages sent from Newfoundland to Ireland on the whole of the sixth day speaks for itself:

"Repeat, please."
"Please send slower for the present."
"How?"
"How do you receive?"
"Send slower."
"Please send slower."
"How do you receive?"
"Please say if you can read this?"
"Can you read this?"
"Yes."
"How are signals?"
"Do you receive?"
"Please send something."
"Please send V's and B's."
"How are signals?"

There was similar confusion over the sending of the signals. Whereas Thomson wished to use low-voltage batteries to provide power for signaling, Whitehouse insisted on employing the huge induction, or spark, coils he had built, which were five feet long and developed at least 2,000 volts. The use of these coils was to result in a great deal of public controversy when the cable finally failed, and there can be little doubt that they helped to break down the faulty insulation.

It was nine days before a single word got through the cable from east to west, but on the twelfth day (August 16) the line was working well enough to start transmitting the 99-word message of greetings from Queen Victoria to President Buchanan. It took sixteen and a half hours before the message was completed; today, it would arrive in America nearly as quickly by airmail.

The first commercial message ever telegraphed across the Atlantic was sent the next day (August 17), from Newfoundland to Ireland. It is one which we can still fully appreciate: "Mr. Cunard wishes telegraph McIver Europa collision Arabia. Put into St. John's. No lives lost."

More days went by while the operators struggled to keep in contact and to transmit the messages which were piling up at either end. Sometimes a personal note intruded, as when Newfoundland remarked plaintively to Ireland, "Mosquitoes keep biting. This is a funny place to live in—fearfully swampy" or when Thomson, no doubt after turning the Valentia office upside down, was forced to ask Newfoundland, "Where are the keys of the glass cases and drawers in the apparatus room?" (The helpful answer: "Don't recollect.")

Finally, after Newfoundland had signaled, "Pray give some news for New York, they are mad for news," the first press dispatch was successfully sent on the twenty-third day (August 27). It is interesting to compare the headlines of 1858 with those of a hundred years later: "Emperor of France returned to Paris Saturday. King of Prussia too ill to visit Queen Victoria. Her Majesty returns to England 30th August. Settlement of Chinese question. Chinese empire open to trade; Christian religion allowed; foreign diplomatic agents admitted; indemnity to England and France. Gwalior insurgent army broken up. All India becoming tranquil."

The last coherent message passed through the cable at 1:30 P.M. on September 1; it was the message to Cyrus Field at the banquet in his honor in New York, and it asked him to inform the American government that the company was now in a position to forward its messages to England.

Thereafter, all was silence. After their brief union, the continents were once more as far apart as ever. The Atlantic had swallowed up the months of toil, the 2,500 tons of cable, the £350,000 of laboriously raised capital.

The public reaction was violent, and those who had been most fervent in their praise now seemed ashamed of their earlier enthusiasm. Indeed, it was even suggested that the whole affair had been a fraud of some kind—perhaps a stock manipulation on the part of Cyrus Field. One Boston newspaper asked in a trenchant headline, "Was it a hoax?" and an English writer proved that the cable had never been laid at all.

What had been hailed as the greatest achievement of the century had collapsed in ruins; it was to be eight long years before Europe and America would speak to each other again across the bed of the ocean.

[Agitation over the failure, coupled with a subsequent cable failure, this time of a line through the Red Sea to India financed by the British government, led to the appointment of a commission of inquiry, with four members nominated by Britain's Board of Trade and four by the Atlantic Telegraph Company.

One of the Board of Trade members was George Parker Bidder, who in addition to being a distinguished engineer was also a mathematical prodigy. At the age of ten he was asked how many times a wheel 5 feet 10 inches in circumference would revolve in running 800,000,000 miles. In less than a minute he had the answer: "724,114,285,704 times with 20 inches left over." He retained this remarkable ability throughout his life. When he was past seventy a friend commented on the number of light vibrations that must hit the eye every second, if there were 36,918 waves of red light in every inch and light travels 190,000 miles a second. "You needn't work that out," Bidder replied. "The number is 444,433,651,200,000."

Altogether Bidder and his fellow judges on the commission sat for nine months—from December, 1859, to September, 1860. Before them paraded a great variety of witnesses—admirals, engineers, businessmen, cable contractors, scientists—each with his own explanation as to why the Atlantic cable had failed or his own suggestion for laying a new one successfully.

Two of the key witnesses were Dr. Whitehouse and Professor Thomson. Whitehouse refused to admit that his theories had been mistaken or that his high-voltage induction coils had contributed to the breakdown of the cable. He did, however, make one valid point: that Cyrus Field had been in so much of a hurry to get on with the laying of the cable that Whitehouse had not had sufficient time for his experiments.

Thomson, who more than any one man was responsible for changing cable engineering from a jumble of theories to an exact mathematical science, had tried unsuccessfully to defend Whitehouse from the wrath of the Atlantic Telegraph Company's directors; but now, criticizing Whitehouse's patent relay, he said: "I find altogether two or three words and a few more letters that are legible, but the longest word which I find correctly given is the word 'be.'" Nevertheless, the committee's report was optimistic: "The failures of the existing submarine lines which we have described have been due to causes which might have been guarded against had adequate preliminary investigation been made into the question," it said, "and we are convinced that if regard be had to the principles we have enunciated in devising, manufacturing, laying and maintaining submarine cables, this class of enterprise may prove as successful as it has hitherto been disastrous."

But the problem of raising money for another attempt seemed insurmountable. Before the committee the secretary of the Atlantic Cable Company had re-

was £600,000 in the bank, only about one-tenth of it from U.S. sources. The next attempt would be largely a British effort.]

The next problem was to decide the design of the new cable. This time there was no headlong rush to get it manufactured and laid before proper tests had been carried out; everyone knew what that policy had cost. Scores of samples were examined and submitted to every conceivable electrical and mechanical ordeal; the design finally approved had a conducting core three times as large as the 1858 cable and was much more heavily armored. It could stand a breaking strain of eight tons, compared with only three for the previ-

As part of New York City's celebration honoring Cyrus Field on the completion of the 1858 cable, firemen parade through Union Square past a statue of Washington in the eerily flickering light of exploding fireworks.

counted his efforts to raise capital among British businessmen. "We have no doubt induced a great many persons to subscribe," he said, "but they do so as they would to a charity, and in sums of corresponding amount. . . ."

Between 1861 and 1864, Cyrus Field had similar troubles in America. In addition to the distrust engendered by earlier cable failures, American financiers were now caught up in the Civil War; England's apparent friendliness to the Confederacy did not make Field's task any easier. Nevertheless, by 1864, there

ous cable, and was over an inch in diameter. Though it weighed one and three-quarter tons per mile, and was thus almost twice as heavy as its ill-fated predecessor, its weight when submerged in water was considerably less. This meant that the strain it would have to bear while being laid was also reduced, owing to the increased buoyancy. Indeed, ten miles of it could hang vertically in water before it would snap under its own weight; this was four times as great a length as would ever be suspended from a cable ship sailing across the North Atlantic, where there could

In an 1858 Leslie's *cartoon Father Neptune receives a nasty shock from the cable.*

never be more than two and a half miles of water beneath the keel.

In every respect, the new cable was a vast improvement over any that had been built before. And yet, despite all the thought, skill, and care that had gone into its construction, hidden within it were the seeds of future disaster.

By the end of May, 1865, the 2,600 miles of cable had been completed. The earlier cable had required two ships to lay it. But this time, by one of history's fortunate accidents, the only ship in the world that could carry such a load was looking for a job. In the Atlantic cable, the fabulous *Great Eastern* met her destiny and at last achieved the triumph that she had so long been denied.

This magnificent but unlucky ship had been launched seven years before, but had never been a commercial success. This was due partly to the stupidity of her owners, partly to the machinations of John Scott Russell, her brilliant but unscrupulous builder, and partly to sheer accidents of storm and sea.*

* James Dugan's book *The Great Iron Ship* is a valuable and highly entertaining history of this wonderful vessel, but unfortunately reports the legend that the skeleton of a riveter was found inside her double hull when she was broken up. This story is much too good to be true, and isn't. Dugan is also far too kind to Russell, whose evil genius not only laid a burden on the *Great Eastern* from which she never recovered, but undoubtedly contributed to the death of her designer. For this side of the story, see L. T. C. Rolt's important biography, *Isambard Kingdom Brunel.*

Nearly seven hundred feet long, with a displacement of 22,500 tons, the *Great Eastern* was not exceeded in size until the *Lusitania* was launched in 1906—48 years later. She was the brain child of Isambard Kingdom Brunel, the Victorian era's greatest engineering genius —perhaps, indeed, the only man in the last 500 years to come within hailing distance of Leonardo da Vinci. Brunel built magnificent stone and iron bridges which are standing to this day (the Clifton Suspension Bridge at Bristol is his most famous, though it was completed after his death) and threw superbly landscaped railways over most of southern England.

Of all his feats, the *Great Eastern* was his last and mightiest. Though *five times* the size of any other ship in the world, she was no mere example—as some have suggested—of engineering megalomania. Brunel was the first man to grasp the fact that the larger a ship, the more efficient she can be, because carrying capacity increases at a more rapid rate than the power needed to drive the hull through the water. (The first depends on the cube of the linear dimensions, the second only on the square.)

Having realized this, Brunel then had the courage to follow the mathematics to its logical conclusion and designed a ship that would be sufficiently large to carry enough coal for the round trip to Australia. (Little more than a decade before, learned theoreticians had "proved" that it was impossible for a steam-driven vessel even to cross the Atlantic.)

With her five funnels, six masts, and superb lines, the *Great Eastern* still remains one of the most beautiful ships ever built, though the absence of a superstructure makes her look a little strange to modern eyes. It is impossible to write of her without using superlatives; her 58-foot paddle wheels and 24-foot screw have never been exceeded in size, and now never will be. This dual-propulsion system made her the most maneuverable ocean liner ever built; by throwing one wheel into reverse, she could rotate around her own axis as if standing on a turntable.

By 1865, the *Great Eastern* had bankrupted a succession of owners and had lost well over a million pounds. Put up at auction without reserve, the floating white elephant was knocked down for a mere £25,000—about a thirtieth of her original cost. The buyers, headed by Daniel Gooch, chairman of the Great Western Railway, had already arranged with Cyrus Field to use the ship for laying the new cable; they were so confident she could do it that they had offered her services free of charge in the event of failure.

To provide storage space for the huge coils of wire, three great tanks were carved into the heart of the ship. The drums, sheaves, and dynamometers of the laying mechanism occupied a large part of the stern decking, and one funnel with its associated boilers had been removed to give additional storage space. When the ship sailed from the Medway on June 24, 1865, she carried 7,000 tons of cable, 8,000 tons of coal, and provisions for 500 men. Since this was before the days of refrigeration, she also became a seagoing farm. Her passenger list included one cow, a dozen oxen, twenty pigs, 120 sheep, and a whole cackling poultry yard of fowl.

Many of the pioneers—one might say survivors—of the earlier expeditions were aboard. Among them were Field himself (the only American among 500 Britishers); Professor Thomson; Samuel Canning, chief engineer of the Telegraph Construction and Maintenance Company; and C. V. de Sauty, the company's electrician. Commanding the ship was Captain James Anderson, but in all matters relating to the cable-laying Canning had supreme authority. Dr. Whitehouse was not aboard, even as a passenger.

This time, with all the cable for the entire job in a single ship, there was no problem of splicing in mid-Atlantic; the *Great Eastern* would sail straight from Ireland to Newfoundland. Thanks to the presence on board of Sir W. H. Russell, the famous war correspondent of the London *Times,* we have a complete record of the voyage, which was later published in a splendidly illustrated volume with lithographs by Robert Dudley.

The shore end of the cable was landed at Foilhommerum Bay, a wild and desolate little cove five miles from Valentia Harbor. The shore end was spliced aboard the *Great Eastern,* and on the evening of July 23, 1865, she turned her bows toward her distant goal. The escorting warships *Terrible* and *Sphinx,*

which had ranged up alongside, and sent their crews up into the shrouds and up to the tops to give her a parting cheer, delivered their friendly broadsides with vigour, and received a similar greeting. Their colours were hauled down, and as the sun set, a broad stream of golden light was thrown across the smooth billows towards the bows as if to indicate and illumine the path marked out by the hand of heaven. The brake was eased, and as the *Great Eastern* moved ahead, the machinery of the paying-out apparatus began to work, drums rolled, wheels whirled, and out spun the black line of the cable, and dipped in a graceful curve into the sea over the stern wheel. . . .

As Russell remarked, "happy is the cable-laying that has no history." This laying was to have altogether too much. The next morning, 84 miles out, the testing instruments indicated an electrical fault at some distance from the ship. There was nothing to do but haul the cable aboard until the trouble was found.

At first sight, this would seem to be a fairly straightforward operation. But with the *Great Eastern,* as she was now fitted out, it was nothing of the sort. She could not move backwards and pick up cable over the stern, where it was paying out, because she would not steer properly in reverse and also because of the danger of the cable fouling her screw. So the cable had to be secured by wire tackle, cut, and transferred the 700 feet to the bow. As Russell describes it:

Then began an orderly tumult of men with stoppers and guy ropes along the bulwarks, and in the shrouds, and over the boats, from stem to stern, as length after length of the wire rope flew out after the cable. The men . . . were skilful at their work, but as they clamoured and clambered along the sides, and over the boats, and round the paddle-boxes, hauling at hawsers, and slipping bights, and holding on and letting go stoppers, the sense of risk and fear for the cable could not be got out of one's head.

It took ten hours to haul in as many miles of cable. When the fault was discovered, it was a very disturbing one. A piece of iron wire, two inches long, had been driven right through the cable, producing a short-circuit between the conducting core and the sea. It might have been an accident; but it looked very much like sabotage.

A new splice was made and paying out started again. This time only half a mile had gone overboard before the cable went dead. Russell remarked despairingly:

Such a Penelope's web in 24 hours, all out of this single thread, was surely disheartening. The cable in the fore and main tanks answered to the tests most perfectly. But that cable which went seaward was sullen, and broke not its sulky silence. Even the gentle equanimity and confidence of Mr. Field were shaken in that supreme hour, and in his heart he may have sheltered the thought that the dream of his life was indeed but a chimera. . . .

Luckily, the fault cleared itself; almost certainly it did not lie in the cable, but in the instruments or connections either at Valentia or aboard the ship. "The index light suddenly reappeared on its path in the testing room, and the wearied watchers were gladdened by the lighting of the beacon of hope once more."

On the fourth day, July 26, the *Great Eastern* ran into heavy seas, which made it hard for the *Sphinx* and the *Terrible* to keep up with her. As she forged ahead at a steady six knots, hardly affected by the waves which battered her little escorts, the *Sphinx* slowly dropped astern and at last disappeared from view. This was a serious loss to the expedition, because owing to some oversight the *Sphinx* carried the only set of sounding gear.

The *Great Eastern* plowed on across the waves, spinning out her iron-and-copper thread.

There was a wonderful sense of power in the Great Ship and in her work; it was gratifying to human pride to feel that man was mastering space, and triumphing over the wind and waves; that from his hands down into the eternal night of waters there was trailing a slender channel through which the obedient lightning would flash forever instinct with the sympathies, passions, and interests of two mighty nations.

On the afternoon of the seventh day, when 716 miles had been paid out, the alarms went again. The fault was close to the ship, so once more the cable was cut, secured by wire ropes, and hauled round to the bow for picking up.

Thousands of fathoms down we knew the end of the cable was dragging along the bottom, fiercely tugged at by the *Great Eastern* through its iron line. If the line or cable parted, down sank the cable forever. . . . At last our minds were set at rest; the iron wire rope was at length coming in over the bows through the picking up machinery. In due but in weary time, the end of the cable appeared above the surface, and was hauled on board and passed aft towards the drum. The stern is on these occasions deserted; the clack of wheels, before so active, ceases; and the forward part of the vessel is crowded with those engaged on the work, and with those who have only to look on . . . the two eccentric-looking engines working the pickup drums and wheels make as much noise as possible . . . and all is life and bustle forward, as with slow unequal straining the cable is dragged up from its watery bed.

It required nineteen hours of this nervous work before the fault was reached—though it would have taken only a few minutes if suitable equipment had been installed at the stern. The cable was respliced, paying out commenced once more, and a committee of inquiry started to examine the faulty coils piled on deck.

Concern changed to anger when it was found that the cable had been damaged in precisely the same manner as before, by a piece of wire forced into it. "No man who saw it could doubt that the wire had been driven in by a skilful hand," Russell comments, and it was pointed out that the same gang of workmen had been on duty when the earlier fault occurred. The sabotage theory seemed virtually proved, and a team of inspectors was at once formed so that there would always be someone in the cable tank to keep an eye on the workmen.

On the morning of August 2, the *Great Eastern* had completed almost three-quarters of her task.

Cyrus Field was one of the watchers on duty in the cable tank that morning. About 6 A.M. there was a grating noise and one of the workmen yelled, "There goes a piece of wire!" Field shouted a warning, but it did not reach the officer at the paying-out gear quickly enough. Before the ship could be stopped, the fault had gone overboard.

This time, it was not a complete short-circuit; the cable was usable, but no longer up to specification. Though Professor Thomson thought it could still transmit four words a minute—which would be enough to make it pay its way—Chief Engineer Canning decided not to take a risk. If he completed the cable, and the customer refused to accept it, his company would be ruined.

In any case, picking up a faulty section of cable was now a routine matter; the men had had plenty of practice on this trip. Canning had no reason to doubt that after a few hours delay, the *Great Eastern* could continue on the last 700 miles of her journey.

The cable was cut, taken round to the bows, and the hauling-up process began again. While this was going on, one of the workmen in the tank discovered some broken armoring wires on the piece of cable that had been lying immediately below the faulty section; the iron was brittle and had snapped under the tremendous weight of the coils above it. This, said Russell, "gave a new turn to men's thoughts at once. What we had taken for assassination might have been suicide!"

The *Great Eastern* was now over waters 2,000 fathoms deep, though the exact depth was not known, owing to the absence of the *Sphinx* with the only set of sounding gear. From the start, the picking-up process failed to go smoothly. First the machinery gave trouble; then the wind made the *Great Eastern* veer around so that the cable did not come straight over the sheaves. It started to chafe against the ship, and when the picking-up machinery began to work once more, the strain on the cable proved too great for the weakened portion. "The cable parted . . . and with one bound flashed into the sea. . . . There around us lay the placid Atlantic, smiling in the sun, and not a dimple to show where lay so many hopes buried."

[Now began a lonely and dramatic battle in the middle of the ocean. With a five-pronged grapnel the *Great Eastern* began to probe the Atlantic ooze two and a half miles down, fishing for the severed cable. Having no single line long enough to reach the ocean floor, the ship's officers improvised one from two dozen sections of wire rope, each 600 feet long, joined together by shackles. Twice the cable was hooked and brought part way to the surface, but each time a shackle broke and the ponderous cable sank again. Crew members did succeed, however, in dropping a buoy to mark their position, and this was to prove exceedingly useful later on. On the third try the line twisted in one of the grapnel's flukes and the grapnel came up empty.]

The fourth attempt was made the next day, and on the afternoon of August 11, the cable was hooked again.

When the cable broke in 1865 the Great Eastern *dropped this buoy, then returned in 1866 and raised the cable.*

Harper's Weekly, SEPTEMBER 30, 1865

It was too much [wrote Russell] to stand by and witness the terrible struggle between the . . . hawser, which was coming in fast, the relentless iron-clad capstan, and the fierce resolute power in the black sea. . . . But it was beyond peradventure that the Atlantic Cable had been hooked and struck, and was coming up from its oozy bed. What alternations of hopes and fears! . . . Some remained below in the saloons, fastened their eyes on unread pages of books, or gave expression to their feelings in fitful notes upon piano or violin. . . . None liked to go forward, where every jar of the machinery made their hearts leap into their mouths. . . .

It was dark and raw that evening, and after dinner Russell left the saloon and walked up and down the deck under the shelter of the ship's paddle box.

I was going forward when the whistle blew, and I heard cries of "Stop it!" in the bows, shouts of "Look out!" and agitated exclamations. Then there was silence. I knew at once that all was over. The machinery stood still in the bows, and for a moment every man was fixed, as if turned to stone. Our last bolt was sped. The hawser had snapped, and nigh two miles more of iron coils and wire were added to the entanglement of the great labyrinth made by the *Great Eastern* in the bed of the ocean. . . .

There was a profound silence on board the Big Ship. She struggled against the helm for a moment as though she still yearned to pursue her course to the west, then bowed to the angry sea in admission of defeat, and moved slowly to meet the rising sun. The signal lanterns flashed from the *Terrible* "Farewell!" The lights from our paddle-box pierced the night "Good-bye! Thank you," in sad acknowledgment. Then each sped on her way in solitude and darkness.

The 1865 expedition had been yet another failure—but with a difference. It had proved so many important points that there could no longer be any reasonable doubt that a transatlantic cable could be laid. The *Great Eastern* had demonstrated, through her stability and handling qualities, that she was the perfect ship for the task; the cable itself was excellent, apart from the brittle armoring which could easily be improved—and, most important of all, it had been shown that a lost cable could be found and lifted in water more than two miles deep.

[By early 1866, Field and his British associates had succeeded in raising another £600,000. They ordered 1,600 additional miles of cable (the brittle armoring was replaced by a more ductile covering of galvanized iron), obtained the loan of the H.M.S. *Terrible* from the Admiralty, chartered two more ships, the *Albany* and the *Medway,* and in July were back in Valentia Bay with the *Great Eastern* and the rest of the telegraph fleet, ready for another try.]

On Friday, the thirteenth of July, 1866, the *Great Eastern* sailed again from Valentia Bay. Those who disliked the date were reminded that Columbus sailed for the New World on a Friday—and arrived on one.

At a steady and uneventful five knots, Brunel's masterpiece plodded across the Atlantic, paying out the cable with clockwork regularity. The only incident on the entire fourteen days of the voyage was when the cable running out from the tank caught in an adjacent coil, and there was a tangle which caused a few anxious moments before it was straightened out.

In England, where the progress of the expedition was known at every minute, excitement and confidence mounted day by day. In the United States, however, it was different, for there was no news of what was happening, nor could there be until the ships actually arrived—if they did. Some spectators were waiting hopefully in Newfoundland, but, as Henry Field remarks,

not so many as the last year, for the memory of their disappointment was too fresh, and they feared the same result again.

But still a faithful few were there who kept their daily watch . . . it is Friday morning, the 27th July. They are up early and looking eastwards to see the day break, when a ship is seen in the offing. Spy-glasses are turned towards her. She comes nearer—and look, there is another and another. And now the hull of the *Great Eastern* looms all glorious in that morning sky. They are coming! Instantly all is wild excitement. The *Albany* is the first to round the point and enter the bay. The *Terrible* is close behind. The *Medway* stops an hour or two to join on the heavy shore-end, while the *Great Eastern,* gliding calmly in as if she had done nothing remarkable, drops her anchor in front of the telegraph house, having trailed behind her a chain of two thousand miles, to bind the old world to the new.

No name could be more appropriate than that of the landing place—Heart's Content. "Heart's Content was chosen now because its waters are still and deep, so that a cable skirting the north side of the Banks of Newfoundland can be brought in deep water almost till it touches the shore. All around the land rises to pine-crested heights; and here the telegraph fleet, after its memorable journey, lay in quiet, under the shadow of the encircling hills."

The triumph was marred by a slight annoyance; the St. Lawrence cable had been broken, and so there was a delay of two days before the telegraph connection could be completed to the United States. It was not until the morning of Sunday, July 29, that New York received the message: "Heart's Content, July 27. We arrived here at 9 o'clock this morning. All well. Thank God, the cable is laid and in perfect working order. Cyrus W. Field."

[But Cyrus Field was not finished. As soon as the *Great Eastern* could be refueled, she and the rest of the telegraph fleet rendezvoused in the Atlantic near the buoy marking the spot where the 1865 cable had parted. Then began a grueling effort to hook and raise the severed cable. On the thirtieth attempt success was achieved. The *Great Eastern* had brought 600 miles of cable from Newfoundland; this was spliced to the recovered line and the great ship turned westward again, bringing her second transatlantic cable into Heart's Content only four weeks after she had arrived with the first. "The long and weary battle was ended," Mr. Clarke concludes. "From that day to this, America and Europe have never been out of touch for more than a few hours at a time."]

Arthur C. Clarke, an Englishman, has written extensively on science. He is a former chairman of the British Interplanetary Society and a fellow of the Royal Astronomical Society. Among his nonfiction works are Interplanetary Flight, Exploration of Space, *and* Making of a Moon.

"FROZEN ASSET" OR FORTY-NINTH STATE?
(Congress debates acquiring Alaska, 1867)

REPRESENTATIVE CADWALLADER C. WASHBURN
(on whether to make an appropriation)

"All the evidence we have in regard to the country goes to show its inhospitable and worthless character. . . . [It] will always be a source of weakness. . . . It is proposed to pay $7,200,000 for a country where none but malefactors will ever live, and where we are likely to be at constant war with the savages."

SENATOR CHARLES SUMNER
(advocating ratification of the treaty)

"Small beginnings, therefore, are no discouragement; I turn with confidence to the future. . . . A practical race of intrepid navigators will swarm the coast, ready for any enterprise. . . . Commerce will find new arms, the country new defenders, the national flag new hands to bear it aloft."

Mr. Godey's Lady

CONTINUED FROM PAGE 22

made her a formidable figure. She was a High-Church Episcopalian, and years later, when she had grand-children, one of them remembered that "when dressed for church she was an imposing spectacle, rather like a duchess of fiction."

The magazine that she put together carried poems, stories, and literary criticism—much of it written by Mrs. Hale herself. But what gave it character were the crusades for which its editor soon became famous and which she never abandoned for the remainder of her long editorial career. Her principal campaign, undoubtedly an outgrowth of her own hard experience, was for the education of women and their eventual acceptance into the teaching profession. But she embraced other causes which brought her equal fame.

The first, conducted in 1833, more outside the columns of the *Ladies' Magazine* than within them, was the founding of the Seaman's Aid Society. By improving the wretched life of the mariner, she reasoned, she might in turn better the lot of his wife and children. Since a seaman's family could not subsist on his monthly earnings of $10 to $18 (part of which he might squander for grog), many a wife toiled in a sweatshop for a wage of a dollar or less a week making uniforms, which were then sold to her husband at inflated prices. Conceiving the idea of "the workbasket," Mrs. Hale and her enthusiastic Boston coterie paid seamen's wives much higher wages for uniforms they made and then sold them at cost to the sailors. The plan worked beautifully. Soon the Seaman's Aid Society was operating a store that could not begin to handle the business. The operators of the competing "slop-shops" and the proprietors of the seamen's boardinghouses, who had always received a cut on uniforms they sold to their tenants, protested bitterly but could do little. Seaman's Aid was underselling them.

With the opening of Mariner's House, the first sailors' home, it was clear to all hands that Mrs. Hale and her ladies knew how to steer in heavy weather. With its clean rooms furnished with castoffs from their attics, its wholesome food, and modest prices, Mariner's House was the ladies' antidote for the water-front clip joints. It was the model for all the Snug Harbors that have succeeded it.

Mrs. Hale's next and totally different Boston crusade was the completion of the Bunker Hill Monument. Lafayette had laid the cornerstone in 1825 before a huge concourse of people, while the air rang with patriotic phrases from the lips of Daniel Webster. Within ten years after the dedication, the monument

had risen only eighty feet out of the 220 the architects called for. Its promoters had given up for want of funds, and in Boston a promise to be fulfilled "when the Bunker Hill Monument is finished" became a sorry public joke. But the all-male Monument Association's shame was even hotter when Sarah Hale volunteered the services of her *Ladies' Magazine*.

Declaring that "we offer our assistance as helpers only," she reassured the association that everything would be done with modesty and decorum. The association could not at first bring itself to accept but finally did so in desperation. Ingeniously, Mrs. Hale set up a "committee of correspondence" composed of Boston society women (was this the forerunner of the list of "sponsors"?) and the *Ladies' Magazine* became the first in the country to engage in a public fund-raising campaign. Despite the hard times of the mid-1830's, Mrs. Hale managed to raise $3,000, a significant sum in those days, although far short of her goal. In 1840 (she was now editor of *Godey's* but had not yet moved to Philadelphia) she crowned ten years of effort in behalf of the monument with a great bazaar for which her readers and the Seaman's Aid Society, by then the largest women's organization in the country, had pickled, canned, knitted, and embroidered for months.

Early in September their goods started pouring into Quincy Hall, and in the week of the ninth crowds of thousands, filling aisles, carried away the handiwork of women all over the nation. Mrs. Hale noted the exciting events of the hour in a daily paper called *The Monument*. "On the last night," Richardson Wright has written, "when the final embroidered bertha had been sold, and the remaining hug-me-tight knocked down to the highest bidder, the treasurer announced that the bazaar had rolled up a $30,000 profit. The monument was assured. Boston's honor was saved. Two years later, in 1842, the final capstone was set in place." Mrs. Hale witnessed the ceremony "with gratified and kindling eyes." It was a personal triumph, but it was an even greater one for the thousands of American women she represented. Awareness that they had done something that the men alone had been unable to do had a tremendous effect, not only on women, but on men. Psychologically, the climate for women's organizations and the advancement of women's rights was a little fairer and warmer from that time on.

Not so the prospects for the survival of the *Ladies' Magazine*. Then as now, the staple of most periodicals aimed at women was news of feminine fashions. Mrs. Hale thought it unimportant, and though she was forced to compromise to some extent, she did so reluctantly. Whether for that reason or because of the general financial troubles of the middle 1830's, the *Ladies' Magazine* found itself in difficulty, and Mrs. Hale's appeals failed to persuade her delinquent subscribers to pay their bills.

Help arrived in the person of a plump, genial Philadelphian named Louis Antoine Godey, one of the authentic geniuses of American publishing history. Since 1830 he had been putting out *The Lady's Book,* a potpourri of fiction and poetry, much of it borrowed from English magazines, and "embellishments" like colored fashion plates, illustrations, and songs (sample title: "The Heart of Thy Norah Is Breaking for Thee"). But though Godey was a shrewd businessman with a good idea of what his readers wanted and a determination to give it to them—he originated the idea of special departments on art, cooking, household hints—he was no editor; he needed someone with a point of view to give his magazine

A "manchette," or lace cuff, from an 1847 Lady's Book.

individuality and character. In 1837 he approached Mrs. Hale, offering to buy the *Ladies' Magazine* and install her as editor of the combined publication, to be entitled, somewhat formidably, *Godey's Lady's Book and American Ladies' Magazine.* She accepted.

Under the enterprising Godey as publisher and Sarah Josepha Hale as editor, *Godey's Lady's Book,* as it was soon called, was to gain, over the next forty years, 150,000 subscribers, an astounding total for a women's publication in the middle 1800's. The *Lady's Book* was to become the alpha and omega of the world of women's rights, fashion, etiquette, and cookery. However old-fashioned it may seem today, it was the first successful women's magazine and the direct ancestor of all that have followed it.

Mrs. Hale took over the editor's chair with two strong prejudices: she was opposed to "borrowing" material from other publications, and she still had little use for fashion plates. As for the first, she felt it was a shameful reflection on America that the *Lady's Book* and other U.S. periodicals had been depending so heavily on literary material imported from England. We had good writers here. The *Lady's Book* was going to publish them and, what was more, it was

going to pay substantial rates. While great numbers of dreary stories (some of them her own) appeared under Mrs. Hale's editorship, and dozens of sentimental poems by indefatigable poetesses like Lydia Sigourney, it is not surprising to find also original contributions by Hawthorne, Longfellow, Poe, Dr. Oliver Wendell Holmes, and Harriet Beecher Stowe. Mrs. Hale would pay up to $25 for a poem—a good fee for the time—though James Russell Lowell held out for $30, and got it.

To this policy and the financial outlay it involved, Louis Godey raised no objection. But Mrs. Hale's dislike for fashion plates failed to move him. As early as 1830 a fashion plate had appeared in her own Boston magazine, but she had publicly admitted that "There is no part of our duty as editor of a ladies' Journal which we feel so reluctant to perform, as to . . . exhibit the fashions of dress." She did believe in good grooming, and in her personal appearance was most fastidious in her plain gowns of silk, adorned with costly lace at the neck and wrists. Her readers learned that she disliked earrings and that she made up her own hand lotion of cocoanut milk, rose water, and lard. (What they did not know was that tucked away on the top of her dressing table were brown-paper pads and a bottle of vinegar which she used before retiring to stave off the wrinkles of age.) Mrs. Hale felt that "the result of the finest toilet should be an elegant woman, not an elegantly dressed woman," and despaired of the practice of American designers of imitating "every frippery ornament invented by French and English milliners." Indeed, she wondered why a becoming and convenient mode could not be retained for centuries, thus saving all of the energy, concern, and expense of keeping in style. In despair she wrote:

It is related in history that at the time it was customary for ladies and gentlemen to wear shoes with toes a foot and a half long, and turned up like sleigh runners, the clergy preached a crusade against these ornaments without effect. From hence we may learn that whatever may be said against fashion, it is little more than a waste of time to decry it . . . we are still rocked in fashionable cradles, and buried in fashionable coffins.

If fashion was to be featured she determined to Americanize it, as she had the editorial content. She employed every possible device to do so. Isaac Singer's ingenious new sewing machine was her ally in this cause, for it helped to keep fashion in the home and out of the hands of the *couturiers.* The creaking of treadles and the clacking of shuttles outlining designs suggested by the *Lady's Book* were soon to be heard through every other open window.

It is doubtful if any magazine offered a "shopping

service" before the *Lady's Book*, which first did so 106 years ago. With a view to economy and taste, it volunteered to buy and ship to subscribers almost any article of clothing, including "lingerie," a euphemism popularized by Mrs. Hale. This service must have been the forerunner of the mail-order catalogue. Among other columns that her readers anticipated eagerly each month were those devoted to household hints or aids.

A knitted opera cap.

She pleaded with inventors to produce a competent washing machine. Evidently her prayers were answered, for in April, 1854, she ran a picture of a strange barrel-like device turned by cogwheels and a lever. "For ourselves our spirits fall with the first rising of steam in the kitchen, and only return to natural temperature when the clothes are folded in the ironing basket. We rejoice that a better day is at hand and consider the invention described below as full of deepest interest to our sex as housekeepers."

The *Lady's Book* also illustrated the newest model cottages and modes in furniture, some of them quite ghastly, though Mrs. Hale herself had grown up in—and admired—the good old four-square New England house with its serviceable country furnishings. Like the fashion plates, these seem to have been largely Louis Godey's idea. He once advocated the erection of thatched cottages for indigent farmers. He did not think it necessary to include a barn, since the cow would presumably be in the pasture all summer; in the winter, it could live indoors with the family and help warm the house. In February, 1850, Mrs. Hale warned against the onrushing Victorian era with a prophetic, if oblique, protest against lace curtains. She declared that she enjoyed "the honest sincerity which still lives in the shadow of wall-paper curtains," but felt it her duty to report the advent of lace.

A liberal in conservative clothing like so many others from the rugged and enigmatic New England countryside, Mrs. Hale was sane, practical, and, above all, ingenious in her approach to women's rights. Since any concessions to women obviously had to be made by the men, who were not disposed to make concessions, she used not the axe nor firebrand, but the tools of psychology to achieve her aims. She often began a campaign for her many women's rights projects by admitting that men are the stronger sex.

Men have the mechanical ingenuity which discovers natural laws of science, and how to apply these to their own inventions and constructions. What wonderful talents of power and usefulness God has entrusted to men! And what wonderful things they have done in the world during the last hundred years!

Swelling with pride and magnanimity, her male readers did not sense that they were about to be induced to share some cherished, centuries-old privilege. While such tactics suggest a calculating woman, an appraisal of Mrs. Hale's nature shows that she actually believed in the men as leaders. Although she was interested in freeing woman from her role as a voiceless domestic drudge, she certainly had no notion of interfering with men's prerogatives. Giving woman the rights she pleaded for would be, she insisted, of great value and service to men.

What a vastly more interesting companion and "help-meet" a wife would make, she declared in her campaign for the education of girls and young women, if she were intelligent enough to talk sympathetically with her husband after a day's work. In this light, it appeared to the men that they stood to gain more from the education of women than women themselves did, and they could not justify opposing it.

Mrs. Hale, in other words, had no objection (as did some feminists) to the word "obey" in the marriage ceremony. All she felt was that women ought to be able to read it and write it—for 50 per cent of her generation of women were illiterate. The average woman, a slave to the hearth, was subject always to the caprice of her husband. She could neither hold property nor vote, nor was she considered worthy of an education or even capable of acquiring one.

"The time of action is now," declared Mrs. Hale in November, 1846. "We have only to sow the fields— the harvest is sure. The greatest triumph of this progression is redeeming woman from her inferior position and placing her side by side with man, a *help-meet* for him in *all* his pursuits. . . ." Scarcely an issue of the *Lady's Book* was published during the forty years of her editorship in which she did not have something to say about education for women and in behalf of educated women in schools and colleges as teachers and professors. She warmly supported Emma Willard's pioneer seminary in Troy, New York, helped Matthew Vassar to found his college, and fought for state-supported normal schools.

During the 1840's she gave Elizabeth Blackwell, the

A lady's fur muff.

first woman in the United States to receive a degree in medicine, her most resolute, even militant, support. In the public furor that followed one critic charged Mrs. Hale with attempting to starve men out of the field of medicine. She replied, uncharacteristically, that the men might as well starve as the women. "If men cannot cope with women in the medical profession, let them take an humble occupation in which they can." In 1850 the Female Medical School of Philadelphia, largely her creation, opened its doors. The following year she organized and became president of the Ladies' Medical Missionary Society of Philadelphia. In a glowing editorial about Florence Nightingale she urged that nurses' training schools be established, but the Civil War had long since ended when, in 1873, the first ones were opened.

Meanwhile the persistent editor of *Godey's* was advocating women as clerks in department stores and as waitresses. "Why should women do the harder indoor work of washing, ironing, scrubbing, cooking . . . and men be employed to carry in the food and wait on table? . . . Is such an arrangement just or good? Has not man intruded into woman's sphere in this domestic service?"

But Mrs. Hale was devoted to causes which were not just those of her own sex. She had much to do with the preservation of Mount Vernon as a national shrine and for three decades expended gallons of printer's ink in behalf of Thanksgiving as a national holiday. She had to wait until President Lincoln's administration, when a proclamation from the White House fulfilled her heart's desire.

As the years passed she became more and more critical of the Victorian era and what it was doing to women. Woman needed to be emancipated from her heavy costume. Anyone's health was bound to suffer from imprisonment in all the layers—the flannel petticoat, the under-petticoat, the petticoat wadded to the knees, the white starched petticoat, then the two muslin petticoats, and at length the dress. Mrs. Hale despaired of the wasp waist, hoop skirts, and the swooning parlor-type of lady who wore them. As an antidote she published lessons in calisthenics for ladies and recommended outdoor activities such as the graceful new game of croquet, "Picnics," swimming, and, above all, horseback riding as "beautifying to the human figure." She was sure that "amusements of this sort will do more to restore the

A baby's stocking.

roses to the cheeks of our young girls, faded by a campaign in a winter's ballrooms, than all the doses which the materia medica can suggest."

She was never afraid to fly in the face of fashion—even men's, and in the height of the Victorian era put on a campaign against beards. "Whiskerandos," she called men who wore them, and dismissed the whole fad as an "immense waste of bear's

A "French purse."

grease." Whiskers so hid the faces of those who wore them that a young lady was not able to distinguish her brother from her cousin. Furthermore, "Persons who carry their faces behind a mask of this sort cannot be supposed to possess clear consciences, for honesty and fair-dealing have no motives for any such concealment."

There were limits, however, to the kinds of campaigns Mrs. Hale embarked upon. Some she set herself, others were laid down by Louis Godey. With all her crusading for women's rights, she never came out for women's suffrage. She thought politics was for men, and while she did not attack the suffragettes openly, she did nothing for them. It was also *Lady's Book* policy, as established by Godey, to avoid the discussion of political and social issues—wages and hours, slum conditions, etc. He was no reformer, and even slavery and the oncoming Civil War, the most pressing issues of the time, got scant notice in the magazine. On one occasion southern readers complained—and their complaints got into southern newspapers—because the name of a woman who had written abolitionist articles appeared on the cover of the *Lady's Book* as an editor. Hastily, Louis Godey wrote a letter to the editor of the Columbia, South Carolina, *Telegraph:*

I have been publishing the Lady's Book for twenty years, and *if in that time one line can be found aspersing in any way Southern institutions, I am willing to fall under your censure. . . . I send you a January number. You will see that Grace Greenwood's name is withdrawn from the cover, where it was placed nominally as editor, she never having had the least control of its columns.*

After half a century of public service Mrs. Hale's pen was still busy reviving old causes or introducing new ones: parks and gardens for cities, prison reforms, public playgrounds for children, the abolition of child labor, the placement of women on school boards, the expansion of educational opportunities for the young. When she could no longer go to the offices of the

Lady's Book, she carried on her editorial duties in her daughter's house in a sunny upstairs room with book-lined walls, a wide, chintz-covered sofa on which her grandchildren were always welcome to curl up with a book, and four cages of canaries. In the center was her large table-desk, neatly stacked with papers and manuscripts, a tray which held her gold pen and an inkpot, and a green-shaded student lamp. There was also a dish of grapes—for she considered grapes a health food, so much so that she would often pay outrageous prices to get them out of season.

"I never saw her when she was not working," one of her grandchildren remembered, "except at meals and Sunday nights." Another recalled: "I remember streams of people going upstairs to grandmother's room. Everybody who came to Philadelphia must have called on her."

Mrs. Hale must have practiced what she preached about the raising of children, for hers all distinguished themselves. Her youngest son, William, graduated second in his class at Harvard, became a lawyer in Virginia, and later gained fame as the negotiator for Texas in handling Spanish claims. Another son, Horatio, became a distinguished philologist. David, her eldest son, the youngest in a class of 150 at West Point, died at 25 of illness while serving on the Canadian border. She also financed her two daughters' education at Emma Willard's seminary in Troy. Sarah Josepha, the younger, became a teacher and opened The Boarding and Day School for Young Ladies in Philadelphia.

Mrs. Hale had a generous heart. Other than publishing literary criticism by Edgar Allan Poe, and such of his stories as "The Cask of Amontillado," which appeared for the first time in the *Lady's Book,* she had befriended and helped support the indigent mother of his child-bride. When Mrs. Hale died at 91 she had given away all of her substantial earnings as an editor and author, except $5,000 that Louis Godey had awarded her on the thirtieth anniversary of her editorship of the *Lady's Book.* Somehow she had found time to write some two dozen books, including the 900-page *Woman's Record, or Sketches of All Distinguished Women from 'The Beginning' till A.D. 1850.* Yet of all Mrs. Hale wrote, only "Mary Had A Little Lamb" is really known today.

Sarah Hale and Louis Godey grew old together in their long and mutually pleasant partnership. Godey himself retired from active publishing in August of 1877, after running the *Lady's Book* continuously for 47 years. The following December Mrs. Hale laid down her pen, at the age of ninety. The *Lady's Book* itself, under other directors and other titles, continued until 1898, but it was never the same. For the truth was, as Mrs. Hale's biographer, Ruth Finley, noted:

> The country had grown up with her. The men and women who bore the brunt of the Civil War were being born as she was starting to write. She knew and understood them, and they in turn believed in her. She never expected the impossible; her sympathy with human frailty was too deep for that. . . . Nevertheless, catching sight of goals decades beyond her times, she urged much of striving on her readers and in the main they accepted it. For she was almost invariably right. . . . All the many movements she promoted, all her forward-looking ideas and proposals are now accepted.

Ralph Nading Hill, a native of Vermont, is the author of six books which range from fish (The Window in the Sea) *to fever* (The Doctors Who Conquered Yellow Fever). *He is probably the youngest ex-president of a steamboat company in America—the Shelburne Steamboat Company of Lake Champlain, about which he has written in the April, 1955, issue of* AMERICAN HERITAGE.

Patrolling the Middle Passage CONTINUED FROM PAGE 9

cargo with a spare Brazilian crew and the trade goods to swap for slaves. At the rendezvous the goods went ashore and the Brazilians were exchanged for the largely American crew that had sailed the *Kentucky* out. The two ships then went home in company, the *Kentucky* carrying the slaves and wearing an all-Brazilian character. This gave her no immunity to British search—or American either, under some circumstances. But now she had the *Porpoise* to act as decoy, sizing up any man-of-war that appeared, hoisting a provocative flag and ostentatiously trying to run for it, drawing the cruiser away from the actual slave carrier. If searched herself, the *Porpoise* had no evidence aboard that would lead to condemnation under the equipment clause. It was prettily worked out. But the *Porpoise* was notorious in the slave trade, and while indulging in such antics in 1855, she was seized by U.S.S. *Raritan.* An American judge condemned her just as if she had been laden to the gunwales with every kind of slaving equipment known to man.

It sounds gratifyingly drastic. But even in the unusual cases when slave ships were seized and condemned in federal courts, front-men acting for their former owners often bought them back again. The whole shore phase of the enforcement of antislaving laws was a joke. For all the law's big talk about piracy and the gallows, slaver captains saw the insides of jails only long enough for bail to be raised. The bail was not high, and it was promptly forfeited. Furthermore, United States consuls and customs officials were often strangely unwilling to ask searching questions about the actual ownership and missions of ships known as slavers all over the water front.

At sea, however, the picture was brighter. British and American naval officers respected one another professionally and got on well when their paths crossed off West Africa. Their common distaste for the abuse of American colors sometimes led them to combine operations—as when, in 1840, the commander of U.S.S. *Grampus* arranged to take over from British men-of-war at Sierra Leone any American-flag slavers that they came across; the British would leave the actual search to the American captain, in order not to stir up protest. He in turn would hand over to the British suspected slavers flying any other flag. Presently officers experienced in the West African squadron were asking the Navy Department to sanction "joint-cruising"—H.M.S. *Towser* and U.S.S. *Jonathan* to hunt together, the latter pouncing on anything which hoisted American colors, the former taking care of everything else. But Washington frowned on all such arrangements, adhering instead to the clumsy, ineffectual eighty-gun agreement.

Sometimes an impatient U.S. Navy commander managed to dabble in co-operation with the British without incurring rebuke from his superiors. In 1845 U.S.S. *Truxtun*, Commander Bruce, sent two cutters and twenty-seven men to help H.M.S. *Ardent,* Commander Russell, to raid the slaving depots up the River Pongo. While the two ships lay waiting, the *Truxtun* offered no objection when the *Ardent* fired at an American brigantine to bring her to for inspection; in fact, the two commanders checked her over arm in arm. In due course out of the river came the American slaver *Spitfire*, prize to the *Truxtun*'s cutters, and some while later the Spanish slaver *Dos Hermanos*, prize to the *Ardent*'s boats. Both had been caught red-handed, or perhaps "black-handed" would be more accurate. The *Ardent*, a steamer, then towed both prizes and the *Truxtun* to Sierra Leone, whence a prize crew took the *Spitfire* to the States. The technique was as efficient as it was friendly—a tantalizing example of how much fear of God could have been put into slavers if only Uncle Sam had seen fit to let the two navies handle matters their own way.

American recalcitrance about right-of-search was especially graceless because while British men-of-war had to be so careful about boarding American-flag vessels, U.S. Navy ships were boarding British-flag vessels in both West Indian and West African waters. When British diplomats mentioned these practices, all that their American opposite numbers could do was change the subject.

To judge by their logs U.S. Navy ships even used British colors in approaching suspicious vessels. Explanation is hardly necessary: If British colors on U.S.S. *Jonathan* moved a slaver to hoist American colors as safeguard, the *Jonathan* had her dead to rights and there would be one less slave smuggler on the high seas—for a while anyway. The record fails to mention it, but it would seem that this ruse accounted for the extreme but well-deserved hard luck of Captain Nathaniel Gordon of Portland, Maine.

In 1860 his ship, leaving the West African coast, found herself pursued by a man-of-war, a steamer. Whatever his reason for assuming she was British—perhaps he caught a glimpse of a white ensign—Captain Gordon had good reason to prefer not to be boarded. Up went the Stars and Stripes. The stranger was actually U.S.S. *Mohican*, so this only made her pour on coal. Soon a boat's crew of Captain Gordon's countrymen were calling on him. "Found her to be the ship Erie of New York," says the firmly indited entry in the *Mohican*'s log, "without papers or any person claiming to be captain, and with 893 slaves on board, having a mixed crew of Spaniards, Americans and Frenchmen."

Gordon had obviously followed an old slaver's dodge: He had thrown the ship's papers overboard at the last minute to confuse the issue of jurisdiction. At his trial he denied that he had been in command. His mates swore that a certain Manuel had been in charge. But several seamen testified that it had been Gordon who had given the orders when the *Erie* put to sea after loading the slaves. Worst of all, Gordon's timing was unfortunate. At home the Battle of Bull Run had already been fought, and the atmosphere had so changed that the United States was moving toward a reciprocal search treaty with Britain. Within a few months the treaty was signed, and within two years slaving in *Rebecca*-type operations would be finished.

Thus it happened that Nathaniel Gordon became the first Yankee skipper ever hanged for slaving, though the federal statute which equated slavery and piracy had already been in force for 42 years. It was high time.

J. C. Furnas, who lives in Lebanon, New Jersey, is the author of Goodbye to Uncle Tom, *a study of the impact of* Uncle Tom's Cabin *on the United States. This article is based on Mr. Furnas' research for a forthcoming book entitled* The Road to Harpers Ferry.

Isaac Singer and his Wonderful Sewing Machine

CONTINUED FROM PAGE 38

pective clergymen and missionaries, Clark nevertheless, as we have seen, accepted.

There were now once again three partners—Singer,
Zieber, and Clark—and all three, so unlike in other
ways, were united in one respect: each thought there
was one partner too many. Zieber, the would-be capitalist, considered Clark a usurper. Neither Clark nor
Singer could see that Zieber was of any earthly use.
An open rupture, however, was averted when Zieber
fell sick of undulant fever; in the fear that he might
die and leave a widow harassed by debts, he consented
to sell his interest in the company to Singer and Clark
for $6,000—an adequate return on the $40 he had
originally invested, but microscopic in terms of what
the interest was soon to be worth.*

Clark, once he had decided to stay with the firm
despite Singer's gaudy peccadilloes, turned out to be
precisely the man for the job. By that time he had
discovered (or thought he had) how far the warmth
of Singer's nature could lead him; but he had discovered as well that Singer's machine was so far superior to any other on the market that, if all went
well, he would soon be a very wealthy man indeed.
Despite his wife's advice, then, and to protect his
stake, Clark plunged enthusiastically into the welter
of lawsuits that had been let loose by Elias Howe's
charges of infringement.

By 1852 there were a dozen or more manufacturers
elbowing their way into the sewing-machine business,
each seeking any means, fair or foul, to wring an advantage from the rest. Of these, the largest were I. M.
Singer & Co., Wheeler & Wilson Co., and Grover &
Baker Co. In addition, Howe, although at first he
manufactured no machines, bulked big because of his
patent. From 1852 until late in 1856 each of these
parties zestfully sued every other in what the press
hailed as "the sewing machine war."

It all began quietly enough with a suit brought by

Howe against an unimportant company, but by 1854,
having won a series of minor victories, Howe was able
to force I. M. Singer & Co. to pay $28,000 in settle-
ment of past claims and, furthermore, to pay a license
fee of $10 on every machine sold in the future. By
that time Clark had cunningly purchased the rights
to a number of early patents, in consequence of which
he was ready to bring suit, on behalf of I. M. Singer
& Co., against all his rivals. In October, 1854, Clark
wondered whether, like himself, those rivals might
not be wearying of the struggle. "There are many co-
gent reasons," he wrote to Howe, "why, in the future,
we should act cordially together in respect to the
maintenance and enforcement of our various pat-

This was Singer's original sewing machine, patented in 1851.

ents." But this reasoning failed; he was obliged to
club his mulish competitors over the ears with lawsuits for two more years.

At length, in answer to an action brought by Clark
in a United States circuit court at Albany, New York,
there assembled the officers and counsel of all the
principal sewing-machine manufacturers. Howe was
there too, called as a witness. All the interested parties were stopping at the same hotel, Congress Hall,
and presently all hands were plunged into negotia-
tions. All night they chaffered and bickered, but a
few minutes before the scheduled time for court to
sit on the first of the suits, the disputants smiled,
shook hands, and initialed a memorable agreement.
Under its terms there was established what was called
(the phrase had, at the time, no connotations of re-
straint of trade or competition) the Sewing Machine
Combination. It was the archetypal patent pool, the
model for similar arrangements later agreed upon in

---

* In an account of this incident which he wrote some time later
—for he survived the fever—Zieber was well-nigh incoherent with
rage. He had, he contended, been "robbed," "victimized" by
scoundrels. He claimed that he would never have agreed to sell
out for a paltry $6,000 had not Singer told him: "The Doctor
thinks you won't get over [your sickness]. Don't you want to give
up your interest in the business altogether?" Not until later,
Zieber claimed, did he discover that Singer had never met the
physician and that the physician had never said any such thing.
In his account of the affair, however, Zieber reveals himself to be
a well-meaning but naïve man, pathetically fated to lose out under the economic code of the nineteenth century—survival of the
fittest. "During the month of June, 1860," he wrote, "I disposed
of the stock on hand, and went afterwards to Montevideo."

On March 6, 1865, Singer employees marched in New York's Grand Procession honoring Lincoln's second inauguration.

the automotive, aircraft, movie, and radio industries.

The pool was a triumph for Clark. Not only did it put an end to all the expensive litigation; not only did the four principals—I. M. Singer & Co., Grover & Baker, Wheeler & Wilson, and Elias Howe—agree to cross-license all their patents; additionally, all other sewing-machine manufacturers were obliged to pay a license fee of $15, of which $5 went to Howe, $5 to I. M. Singer & Co., and $2.50 to each of the other companies. Howe's royalty was thus cut in half,* and the primacy of I. M. Singer & Co. as manufacturers was acknowledged. It remained only for Clark, as a merchant, to maintain that position.

To attempt to sell a home appliance a century ago was to brave an uncharted wilderness. How to gain consumer acceptance for a brand-new gadget? How to demonstrate that the owner's life would be enriched by its possession? How high to price this innovation? How to merchandise and distribute profitably, on a nationwide basis? How to evaluate the importance of advertising? What share of profits to plow back for expansion and for research and development? In short, how best and most profitably to sell and keep on selling? These are all questions that intensely interest manufacturers, distributors, salesmen, and their advertising agents today; and it is safe to say that today's entrepreneurs are all following the trail that

* But in return, the others agreed that they would license at least 24 manufacturers. Howe's patent expired in 1860; at that time the license fee was cut to $7, and Howe's share to $1. Considering that his invention had never been practical, he did well from it: his royalties are reported to have totaled $1,185,000. Thanks to his victories in the cases for infringement, moreover, to him has been accorded the accolade of history (at least in the United States) as the inventor of one of the most useful of all home appliances, a device described by Louis Antoine Godey, the publisher of *Godey's Lady's Book,* as "next to the plough . . . perhaps humanity's most blessed instrument."

Clark boldly and resourcefully hacked into the forest. Consider just a handful of the problems Clark faced, and his pioneering solutions.

Item: How to overcome the prevailing prejudice that women were too stupid to be trusted with a machine? As early as 1852 there was a girl in the company's Broadway shopwindow, demonstrating how simple the machine was to operate; the crowds that gathered to watch were as big as any that flocked to Phineas T. Barnum's museum, a few steps away. Moreover, Clark established, all over the country, a fully developed system of franchised agencies, each of which was staffed by an agent who was also the salesman, a young woman to demonstrate the machine, and a competent mechanic to service and repair the machines sold. Such a system was unique in its time. "The business we do is peculiar," Clark wrote in 1853, "and we have adopted our own method of transacting it."

Item: How to persuade the customer who already owned a sewing machine that he should buy an improved model, incorporating new features? By February, 1856, Clark announced that any "inferior or wholly worthless" machine—by which he intended the public to understand any machine that was not a new Singer—could be traded in against a new Singer for a cash value of fifty dollars. This was another first for the sewing-machine industry.

Item: How to influence the market leaders? Clark offered clergymen his machines at half price; newspaper publishers were made the same offer if they would give advertising space to compensate for the other half.

Item: How to sell an appliance costing more than $100 at a time when the American family's average annual income was in the neighborhood of $500? In

September, 1856, Clark, taking his cue from New York furniture manufacturers and New England clockmakers, introduced the concept of installment buying, and this was a first for any merchant distributing on a national scale. It was also a startling innovation in commercial relationships. It so bemused a writer for the *Scientific American* that he lost his grip on his syntax: "A psychological fact, possibly new, which has come to light in this sewing machine business," he wrote, "is that a woman would rather pay $100 for a machine in monthly installments of five dollars than $50 outright, although able to do so."

All this commercial pioneering brought a gratifying flood of the dimes that, Isaac Singer had declared, were all he was after. How could it be otherwise when, for a machine priced at $110, the manufacturing costs ran as low as $23? Singer, with only an occasional show of bravura in the commercial sphere, had sedulously devoted himself to improving the product. He left Clark to attend to the business end: the legal questions, the patent problems, the merchandising and the primitive advertising. Singer was even content to have Clark make his machine fancy; "Mr. Singer," Clark wrote to an agent, "is now fully aroused as to the importance of having highly ornamented machines." Singer himself, meanwhile, poured his energies into product research and development and into production. By 1857 he held a dozen patents on various developments. He had spent long hours in the machine shop; one of the mechanics later recalled him as "companionable . . . a good story teller . . . his genius for acting came into good play. The world was made brighter by his presence."

But Singer considered it was time for him to brighten more of the world than just his machine shop. By 1859 his loves and his comforts, like those Desdemona prayed for, began to increase even as his days did grow. Together with his principal consort, Mary Ann Sponsler, he moved to a fashionable address, 14 Fifth Avenue. The count of his progeny was now eighteen: two by his wife, Maria; ten by Mary Ann Sponsler (but of these two had died); one by Mary Eastwood Walters "Merritt"; and five by Mary McGonigal "Mathews." His confidence, always high, had waxed to the point where he could recognize love even when it came to him under some name other than Mary. He engaged to accept the devotion of a pair of Ellens—Ellen Brazee and Ellen Livingston—young ladies whose unions with Singer were, however, never blessed. Heretofore he had been content to wait for love to come to him, but now he grew apprehensive; he seemed to dread that perhaps love was not aware of his change of address. In any event, according to the subsequent testimony of his coachman, he took to waiting for romance to find him on street corners.

Singer kept his coachman busy. He had ten horses, which had cost him $10,000; he maintained three carriages, at a cost of another $3,000. But all this was not enough. He conceived a jumbo equipage on which he actually took out a patent (Number 25,920). It was, said the New York *Herald,* "a regular steamboat on wheels . . . a monster, having all the conveniences of a modern brownstone front, with the exception of a cooking department." This mammoth, weighing nearly two tons and painted, lest anyone fail to notice it, a vivid canary yellow, could seat 31 passengers, inside and out; it was outfitted with a nursery at the back end, "with beds to put the dear ones to sleep"; a small orchestra could be accommodated in seats on the outside, "with guards enough to keep off all outside barbarians"; it was drawn by nine horses: three cream-colored ones in front, then a light-colored cream between two sorrels, and finally a bay between two large gray wheel horses. "Whether," the *Herald*'s reporter commented with pardonable asperity, "this eccentric turnout is intended for speed, comfort or advertisement, the reader must judge."

For a man of Singer's rumbustious tastes and temperament, New York in the years before the Civil War was a congenial playground. A massive man, exploding with vitality, on easy terms with the theatrical and sporting world, Singer ignored the pretensions of Knickerbocker society and by night delighted instead in the more raffish night spots to which he squired actresses of the day. He cut an impressive swath through an unimpressive society, until at length he came a cropper. As might have been predicted, this came about as a result of his ostentation. It could never have happened to a man with only one horse and carriage.

On August 7, 1860, Singer went for a drive up Fifth Avenue with Mary McGonigal. The sun was benign, his curly beard was combed, and all was right with the world until, to his horror, another of his carriages drew up alongside. In it was sitting Mary Ann Sponsler. She looked his way. Hastily he bade his coachman turn down the next street, but too late; Mary Ann's carriage was at his wheels, and Mary Ann's mouth was angrily open.

This incident was the catalyst. Mary Ann had long been privately grieving over the fact that she, the mother of eight Singer children, was not virtuous in the eyes of society. She insisted that she would never have followed him through the Midwest, never have borne his children, had he not promised to divorce Maria Haley and marry her. What irked Mary Ann was that, by August of 1860, Singer was perfectly free to marry again. Six months before, he had at long last divorced his wife, but though he was living with Mary Ann, he had nonetheless refused to make an honest woman of her. And so, on this particular day, her public berating continued through the streets until at last his carriage pulled away from hers and, mercifully, out of range.

Thereafter, just as today, events crowded upon each other according to fixed ritual. She hurried home, but he was there first; there were words, then blows, then appeals to the police, then the cold, white light of public notoriety. Discreetly, Singer decamped to Europe, accompanied, so declared his furious consort, by Kate McGonigal, younger sister of Mary.

In the offices of I. M. Singer & Co., Edward Clark was understandably scandalized. For months he had been seeking general acceptance of the sewing machine by offering it to community leaders—parsons and teachers—at half price. And this was his reward. He sent off one stinging letter of rebuke after another to his chastened partner. When the Civil War broke out, Clark seemed almost to blame that cataclysm, too, on Singer. "Business is pretty much at a standstill," he wrote. "I am suffering for all the large public show of wealth which you made in 1859 and '60. It was industriously spread abroad that the firm was rich. Now all who are rich are expected to be patriotic and to give liberally. . . . I am called on many times a day to subscribe and am obliged to refuse."

Soon after his return to America in 1861, Singer was served with papers by counsel for Mary Ann Sponsler; this time she was suing him for divorce. It was a curious case: a woman who had lived with him intermittently for a quarter century, who had borne him ten children, yet to whom he had never been married, suing for divorce. Her grounds were that Singer had lived with her as his common-law wife for seven months after his divorce from Maria Haley, and in her complaint she made it clear that she had been brooding powerfully for some time over Singer's iniquities. He was, she declared, "a most notorious profligate"; she had concluded, moreover, that "a more dissolute man never lived in a civilized country." This was drawing a very long bow, but apparently the judge agreed with her, for he awarded her $8,000 a year as temporary alimony—a record for the time—pending a permanent settlement. In a commendable effort to save himself still greater notoriety should the suit be prosecuted further, Singer settled out of court: he bought and furnished her a house in 28th Street, paid her lawyers' fees, and gave her $500 in a lump sum and $50 a week for life or for so long as she

should not marry. Then he wrote a crestfallen and characteristically illiterate letter to his partner:

Mr. Clark, dear sir, My private afairs (though justly merited) hangs heavily upon me and my soul sicends [sickens] at the prospects befor me and for the well fare of all conserned try to make my load of grief as light as posabl. . . .

This done, Singer retired again to Europe.

In France, he found, matters were managed differently and, he considered, rather better. He stopped at a *pension* in Paris owned by the English-born widow of a Frenchman. This lady, Mme Pamela Boyer, had a daughter—intelligent, attractive, tactful, and gay. Her name was Isabella, and neither she nor her mother knew of a reason why she should not become the rich American's mistress. And so not only love but also a measure of peace came to the distracted Singer. For Isabella Boyer seems, altogether, to have been a remarkably able woman. When they came to America in 1863 (Singer had learned that Mary Ann Sponsler had secretly married, which obliged him to come to a new settlement with her), Isabella promptly endeared herself to all of Isaac's children, whether of the left hand or the right; moreover, though Isaac had been divorced, she somehow managed to inveigle an Episcopal rector into solemnizing her union with him.

But this belated access of respectability did not suffice to appease Edward Clark. Too long had the partners rasped on each other; in July, 1863, they rancorously agreed to dissolve the partnership. I. M. Singer & Co. became The Singer Manufacturing Company, but, at Isaac's stipulation, neither was permitted to be president of the new corporation so long as the other should live. There were, however, compensations. Of an original capitalization of 5,000 shares priced nominally at $100 apiece, Clark and Singer each held 2,075; the balance they sold (at $200 apiece) to seventeen officers and employees of the company. The first dividend was declared in October, and within five years those who had paid $200 a share for their stock had gotten $225 in dividends. The golden flood was still only a trickle; the company has never skipped a dividend. One share in 1863 had become by 1958, through splits and stock dividends, 900 shares, worth about $36,000 at the current market price of about $40 a share, during which long time it had paid cash dividends of $131,340.

By the end of the Civil War the corporation began to expand in earnest. By 1867 the first foreign factory had been built, near Glasgow; and already the Singer salesman, America's first world-wide commercial ambassador, was pressing his obstinate finger on the doorbells of the world. Everywhere he carried the Singer name; everywhere he enhanced his own reputation for pertinacity. He was incredibly competitive: once, when a Singer representative shot and killed a Wheeler & Wilson rival in a frontier saloon near Tacoma, Washington, he found he had gone too far, for he was lynched. Jokes (many of them, to our sophisticated ears, unbearably corny) grew up around the Singer salesman and his product as, two generations later, they would grow up around the Tin Lizzie. Thus:

"Why is a Singer Sewing Machine like a kiss?"
"Because it seams so good."

On its centennial, not long ago, The Singer Manufacturing Company was able to hand out instruction booklets in 54 different languages, boast of more than 100,000,000 machines sold, point to fifteen factories —seven in the United States and the others scattered over Europe and South America—and glory in 5,000 Singer sewing centers all over the world.

But even as early as 1863 his holdings afforded Isaac Singer a very comfortable living. It was in February of that year that Ebenezer Butterick, a Yankee tailor, conceived the notion (he was not the first to do so) of making and selling dress patterns; and the success of his venture gave a boost to the entire sewing-machine industry. Singers were being sold, as well, to the Union Army; in 1865, when Singer employees marched in a vast New York parade celebrating Lincoln's second inauguration, their principal sign proclaimed, "We Clothe the Union Armies—While Grant Is Dressing the Rebels."

On the tide of this prosperity, Isaac Singer coasted into a cozy retirement. If Clark had feared that his partner would go on as before, he erred, for though Singer was still in the prime of life, he suddenly became a model of docile domesticity, a doting father and grandfather. He even submitted to baptism at the hands of an Episcopal minister, his sponsors being his Catholic-born wife and an illegitimate son. He essayed first the life of a Hudson River Valley patroon; but by 1867 it was evident that his wife was languishing, away from France, so he moved his family back to Paris, to a sumptuous mansion in the Rue Malesherbes. In honor of their return, they named Isabella's fourth (and Isaac's twenty-second) child Paris Eugene. The last two Singer children were born there as well; but then, concerned for his wife's health as much as by the Franco-Prussian War, Singer removed first to London and finally, in 1872, to Oldway, a great estate in Paignton, near Torquay, a seaside resort on the Channel coast of Devon.

Now, hedged about as he was with all the perquisites of the landed gentry, Singer might have produced a fascinating memoir if only he had been literate. He had to express himself otherwise.

There was a large house on his grounds, but it was not grand enough for Singer. He chose to spread himself. Working closely with architect and builders, he caused to be reared a palace which he dubbed The Wigwam: it was a Greco-Romano-Renaissance effusion, colonnaded inside and out. In design, it leaned chiefly on the Petit Trianon at Versailles. In addition to the usual 115 rooms there was a completely equipped theater, a circular coach house big enough for half-a-hundred carriages, and a vast marble hall with a grand marble and bronze staircase flanked by an enormous painting by David portraying the coronation of another man celebrated for the gratification of his instincts, Napoleon I. For all this, the onetime star of *Reclaimed, or, the Danger of Moderate Drinking* shelled out $500,000 in old-fashioned money.

Here, at last, was the life. Singer, now past 60, puttered through his marble halls. He amused himself with sketches toward the invention of a steel truss. He delighted in entertaining his various children, no matter who their mother. The Sunday supplements had yet to be circulated in Paignton; in consequence, Singer was regarded by his humble neighbors as odd, but friendly and generous. Even excessively so: periodically he launched monstrous entertainments to which all in the countryside were invited. When he died in July, 1875, he was tendered an impressive funeral, with a mile-long procession of 75 carriages and two thousand mourners; flags in Paignton and Torquay stood at half-mast.

In New York City, Edward Clark joined in "sincerely deploring the loss of this distinguished inventor," and at once got himself elected president of the company.

The distinguished inventor was dead, but his genes went marching on. So, in more decorous fashion, did those of Edward Clark, who by 1882 had followed Singer to the grave. In death as in life, Clark's effects were tidily and prudently disposed among his near and dear, who were neither numerous nor clamorous.

Singer's legacy, on the other hand, no matter how carefully he had contrived to order it before he died, caused a scandal as great as any in which he had been involved in life.

Clark's heirs, who have held a dominant share of The Singer Manufacturing Company stock, have used their wealth unexceptionably. The beauty of Cooperstown, New York, testifies to their wisdom, as does the first-rate collection of modern French paintings presently gracing the Sterling and Francine Clark Art Institute in Williamstown, Massachusetts. Their generous support of such institutions as the New-York Historical Society and the Metropolitan Museum of Art is well-known. The family, like its founder, has been uniformly well-bred and well-behaved.

In contrast, Singer's will was bitterly contested from every direction. William and Lillian, his oldest legitimate children, had been given $500 and $10,000 respectively. As far back as 1851 William had disgusted his father by his lack of gumption; "The last two days he spent in the office," Barzillan Ransom said of William, "he was engaged in writing a play for one of the Theatres." Perhaps matters might have gone easier with William had he been an acceptable playwright; but no, he was not even that. Isaac's first wife, Catharine Maria, was likewise morose, for she had been left nothing. The three of them, however, settled for an additional $150,000 paid by the more fortunate heirs. (All the other children were awarded handsome bundles of Singer stock.)

The chief recalcitrant was Mary Ann Sponsler Foster. She had embittered Singer's life and blackened his name. Her own children—save one, John Albert Singer—had turned against her. She had struck a deal with Isaac but concealed from him her violation of it. Now she insisted on $1,000,000, rejected any smaller settlement, and required that her suit be brought in the surrogate's court of Westchester County. In a courtroom crowded with fashionably dressed, scandal-minded onlookers, Mary Ann was her own worst witness. Her attorneys were hard put to find witnesses who would support her, even from among her own children. Only Orson Phelps stepped forward, a figure out of the past, to prate of how, a quarter century before, Singer had spent more time reciting Shakespeare than working on his own invention. At length Mary Ann accepted $75,000, in return renouncing all claims.

The subsequent careers of many of Singer's children recalled the gaudy ways of their progenitor. Of the 22 who survived him, all but six had issue, and they contracted among them 35 marriages. One daughter married Prince Edmond de Polignac and was a friend of Marcel Proust; her musicales were celebrated events in Paris, and when she died she left behind a fund, administered by the *Fondation Singer-Polignac,* to give grants-in-aid to talented artists, musicians, and scientists. Another daughter married the downstart son of an impoverished southern banker, passed her middle years storming the aristocratic citadels of Newport, and retired to the Riviera, where, her husband having died, she engaged a succession of handsome

chauffeurs and eventually dwindled away into a Noel Coward joke.

The true throwback among the Singer children was Paris, who died in 1932 but was immortalized in Isadora Duncan's memoirs as her lover (she called him Lohengrin). Paris inherited his father's splendid stature (6'4"), his father's vitality and animal magnetism, a generous slice of his father's fortune (worth, at Paris' majority, perhaps $15,000,000), and his father's faculty for invention (an electric organ and an internal-combustion engine). He was also capable of the grand gesture. Thus, he paid out $200,000 for an option on the old Madison Square Garden as a gift to Isadora Duncan; but when she was not properly appreciative, he allowed the option to lapse and let the $200,000 gurgle down the drain. When they parted in an emotional thunderstorm, Paris consoled himself by staking Addison Mizner as architect of Palm Beach and by himself becoming that resort's *arbiter elegantiae*; the dissolution of his Florida dreams reduced him to sailing up and down the Nile on chartered dahabeahs.

Thanks to their elders, Singer's grandchildren (there were at least 54) had far less money to spend, and they spent or invested it far more primly—albeit not colorlessly. One shot wild animals in the African veld; one built an unimportant railroad; one made a hobby of attending National Amateur Golf Championships ("It brings out the best in me," asserted Mortimer Singer, Jr.); one married a showgirl who, according to Ziegfeld, had the most beautiful legs in the world; one married a broker, and *her* child, grown to man's estate, in 1922 plunked down a substantial sum of money to back *Time,* then still a struggling infant of a news magazine; one, dying in London, left her will so well hidden that a spiritualist who undertook to locate it by means of its emanations swooned from the strain as he left her premises; one retired as a nun into a French convent.

It is difficult, in surveying this assorted brood, to find a clue to a final judgment of their sire. What was Isaac Singer? Was he merely a Casanova? Was he a Don Juan in the Mozartian sense—a rebel, unscrupulously at war with every convention? Or was he simply an amoral and energetic hooligan blessed with a useful mechanical aptitude?

That there were many women in his life there can be no doubt. That most of them were genuinely fond of him is manifest, and it is the rawest of ironies that, in attempting to assess Singer, we must depend almost entirely on the evidence of the one woman who came to hate him. For the only detailed account of his private life is to be found in the divorce proceedings brought against him by Mary Ann Sponsler. She may be said to have been amply avenged for any hurts he gave her; thanks to her, posterity's picture of Singer is that of a blackguard. Yet surely her account was not disinterested.

A less prejudiced witness might have concluded that Singer, while he was not the most punctilious of men, must have been, more often than not, a charming, likeable vulgarian, bubbling over with animal spirits, with a voracious appetite for life and a ready, if rough, talent for savoring all its delights. And quite apart from what he bequeathed to his children, he gave the world a most useful appliance indeed, the more appropriate since it was the gift of a man who, to put it moderately, must have been aware of the toil necessary to raise and clothe a large family.

Peter Lyon, a New York free-lance writer, contributed "The Master Showman of Coney Island" to the June, 1958, issue of AMERICAN HERITAGE.

Tragedy in Dedham CONTINUED FROM PAGE 57

with a revolver of the type that fired the murder bullet, Vanzetti with one that might have been taken from the murdered paymaster.

Sacco maintained that he had put his revolver in his pocket that afternoon and forgotten about it; Vanzetti said that he carried his for protection. Both statements may have been true. Often the lame excuse is really the truthful one. Yet here were two men, philosophical anarchists, who maintained that the use of force was never justified; during the war, they had become fugitives from military service. Their philosophy denied the use of force, even for self-protection (as it must). Yet when they were picked up, almost by accident, they had on them the weapons of force. If they had not been armed the chances are that they would never have come to trial.

The trial may well have been more unfair than seems apparent in the record. There the most glaring fault is the district attorney's harrying interrogation of the two men as to their beliefs, their lack of patriotism, and their reasons for running away to avoid the draft. That the judge allowed such questioning to go on was outrageous.

Its impropriety stares out of the printed page. Here certainly was error, yet I cannot believe that this was primary in the jury's verdict. The judge's charge seems reasonable enough in cold print. Reading it over twice I could not take exception to it.

I was finally left with the feeling that if I had been on the original jury and heard the evidence that was placed before those men, I should probably have voted with the others. Yet I was not really certain.

Looking back at it now over a lapse of years the case of Sacco and Vanzetti becomes a tragedy in the classical sense. It was no melodrama, as many have seen it, with good neatly divided from evil. Katzmann was as sharp as most district attorneys out for a conviction, a limited man but not a bad one. Judge Thayer could not hide the bias of his obsessions off the bench. He was indiscreet and he was weak, but he made an effort to conduct the trial fairly. Both he and Katzmann believed to their dying day that Sacco and Vanzetti were guilty.

It was not a conspiracy of evil men against noble men, as Maxwell Anderson saw it in his theatrical *Gods of the Lightning*. There was something more, something deeper and more embracing than all the literature about the case. It was in fact fate that was the mover behind the events at the Dedham Courthouse in the spring of 1921. And it was fate in the ironic Greek sense, dwarfing all the participants, ending in inexorable disaster.

Sacco and Vanzetti were figures of Greek tragedy, the doomed king's son become in modern dress two Italian workmen. Fate lurks behind them at each step. Sacco, the regular worker, never misses a day at the factory except that one day of the murder when he goes to Boston for a visa to return to Italy. If he had picked any other day, the factory time clock would have been his alibi. Without him it is agreed Vanzetti could not have been convicted. But on that one day fate sent him to Boston. Fate gave him his singular resemblance to Joe Morelli. Fate engineered the almost accidental arrest of the two men as they were riding on the Brockton streetcar. But for fate Sacco would have been off to his native country in two weeks.

And as in Greek tragedy the hero condemns himself unknowingly in his own words, is doomed by his own inner weakness, so in the end are Sacco and Vanzetti doomed by theirs. The men of peace go armed. Fate plus human weakness—that is the basis of high tragedy, a tragedy such as theirs that they played out to the end with bravery and dignity. It was a tragedy for everyone concerned with the case, and in the end it is best accepted so, as it was by the Greeks.

Francis Russell has written on Boston's Shirley Mansion and on the colonial missionary John Eliot for previous issues of AMERICAN HERITAGE.

Was John Smith a Liar?

CONTINUED FROM PAGE 33

reputation with historians is concerned, she has done even more for him than Pocahontas.

Her name is Laura Polanyi Striker. Born in Vienna and trained at the University of Budapest, Dr. Striker was an editor and lecturer before coming to America. At the request of some of her academic colleagues she examined Smith's Hungarian story and Kropf's interpretation of it. Her findings, which are just being made known to the historical world, put Captain Jack back in the running as an honest man.*

What were the essential features of the Hungarian story, and how much of it can be checked against the existing record?

Smith claimed that he went to Hungary in 1601, hoping to fight against the Turks. When he got to Graz, Austria, he found an English Jesuit who introduced him to "Lord Ebersbaught." Impressed by Smith's mastery of a pyrotechnical signal system, "Ebersbaught" introduced him to "Baron Kissell," who in turn gave him a hearing with "Henry Volda, Earl of Meldritch." These were the chief actors in Smith's dramatic story.

Because he could find mention of none of these people in the archives, Kropf had called Smith a liar. But Dr. Striker, more meticulous and ingenious in her scholarship, has located them all. The English Jesuit, she discovered, was William Wright. "Ebersbaught" was Carl von Herbertsdorf. "Kissell" was Hanns Jacob Khisl, Baron of Kaltenbrunn, court war counselor of the Archduke Ferdinand. "Volda" was actually Folta—one of a number of noble families which had been given domains near the place where the battles Smith described were fought. In 1602, wrote Smith, "Volda" completed his twentieth year in military service—and Dr. Striker has found confirmation of this. Smith knew what he was talking about, even to the smallest detail. The people he names did indeed exist. The truth was that Smith, like so many Englishmen before and since, had a genius, if not a passion, for misspelling foreign names.

Smith tells how "Ebersbaught" was besieged by the Turks at "Olumpaugh" (Oberlimbach). When "Kissell" came forward to break the siege, claims Smith, he was

able to use pyrotechnics and get this message across: "On Thursday night I will charge to the East. At the Alarum, salley you." Another of Smith's fireworks tricks made the Turks think they were being attacked on the left. When they rushed troops there, "Kissell" attacked on the right, and the Turks were overrun.

All this sounded to Kropf like pure fiction. Not so. As the re-examination of the case continued, Dr. Franz Pichler, counselor of the Styrian Archives, decided to re-enact the event on the terrain, and with pyrotechnics, such as Smith might have used. So far as he could determine, it would have been quite possible for Smith to have done just what he claimed.

Later on, when he went with "Volda" into Transylvania, Smith says he reported not to the Austrian but to the Transylvanian commander, Sigismund. Why the "unexplainable" switch in loyalty? Dr. Striker has explained it. "Volda's" estates were in Protestant Transylvania. The Austrians were fanatically pro-Catholic, and Protestants were not allowed to fight in the Imperial Army. It seems not at all unreasonable that "Volda" might have had a grudge against the Austrians, thrown in his lot with Sigismund, and taken his new friend, Smith, with him.

Next comes the most puzzling detail of all. Smith says that under Sigismund he and "Volda" fought "some Turks, some Tartars, but most Bandittoes, Rennegadoes, and such like." How could this be, when the enemies of Sigismund's Transylvanians were not the Turks, but the Austrians?

Again Dr. Striker has been able to disentangle the confusing skein of Hungarian history. Sigismund had made a special agreement with the Austrian General Basta to drive out of the country an army of Hajdus, a people of Turkish-Hungarian stock whose polyglot mercenary troops were plaguing the region. Unable to control them himself, Basta promised Sigismund a truce if he would do the job. Kropf failed to find proof that this agreement existed, and concluded that Smith was a liar. Actually, Smith knew enough to place these Hajdus in exactly the right spot and at the right time, as the documents proved.

Unable to dislodge the Hajdus from their fortress, Sigismund's troops camped outside the walls, from which their enemies taunted them. Finally, a Hajdu fighter sent a challenge for a trial at arms. Smith met the warrior, defeated him, and cut off his head. He did the same to two others. When the heads were presented to the General, Smith was rewarded with a "faire horse richly furnished, a Semitere, and belt worth three hundred ducats." He even got a coat of arms for his valor.

Highly improbable, Smith's enemies have always

* See Dr. Striker's article, "Lewis L. Kropf on Captain John Smith's True Travels," *Virginia Magazine of History and Biography*, January, 1958; and Dr. Striker's contribution to *Captain John Smith, His Life and Legend*, by Bradford Smith.

SPECIAL CHRISTMAS GIFT RATES

$12.50 for your own new subscription or your first gift subscription for one year—six issues. (You save $5.20 under the cost of the same six issues at the retail price—$2.95 each.)

$10.95 for each additional gift subscription or for *all* of them if you are already an AMERICAN HERITAGE subscriber yourself. (You save $6.75 under the retail price.)

These rates apply only for Christmas gifts within the U.S. For outside the U.S. please add $1.00 for each subscription.

SPECIAL CHRISTMAS GIFT ARRANGEMENTS

Unlike the average magazine present at Christmas, AMERICAN HERITAGE will be delivered *before* the holiday and the gift card with your name as donor *will accompany it.*

Your gift will be handsomely packaged, with a "Do Not Open Until Christmas" label; and an attractive announcement card, hand-signed as you direct, will be attached to the carton.

With the gift card will be an extra present, a folded 1½ by 2 feet reproduction of a famous map of early America: "The New Netherlands and New England, 1635." This is a striking full-color gravure print of a richly illuminated and oddly oriented map ("North" is to the right, rather than at the top), drawn by the Dutch cartographer Willem Janszoon Blaeu. There is *no extra charge* for the map.

NOTE: We cannot promise pre-Christmas delivery for late orders. Mail may be slow during the holiday season. So there's good reason to mail this postage paid form as promptly as possible—today if you can.

AMERICAN HERITAGE
Christmas Order Form

SPECIAL HOLIDAY GIFT RATES

ONE SUBSCRIPTION $12.50 · EACH ADDITIONAL GIFT $10.95

Please send a year of AMERICAN HERITAGE as my gift —

1 $12.50
OR $10.95 ✱

TO _____
please print

STREET & NUMBER _____

CITY _____ ZONE _____ STATE _____

SIGN GIFT CARD "FROM _____ "

2 $10.95

TO _____
please print

STREET & NUMBER _____

CITY _____ ZONE _____ STATE _____

SIGN GIFT CARD "FROM _____ "

3 $10.95

TO _____
please print

STREET & NUMBER _____

CITY _____ ZONE _____ STATE _____

SIGN GIFT CARD "FROM _____ "

FOLD — MAIL TODAY

☐ I ENCLOSE $_____   ☐ BILL ME LATER

for _____ subscriptions.

MY NAME _____
please print

STREET & NUMBER _____

CITY _____ ZONE _____ STATE _____

✱ **4**

☐ Check here if you are already a subscriber yourself. Subscribers are entitled to the $10.95 rate for all Christmas gifts.

☐ Enter my own NEW subscription for $12.50 as part of this order, making the rate on all my Christmas gifts $10.95 each.

TO INSURE PRE-CHRISTMAS DELIVERY OF THE FIRST ISSUE ACCOMPANIED BY YOUR GIFT ANNOUNCEMENT CARD, MAIL THIS FORM TODAY declared. Ridiculous, said Kropf. Yet a seventeenth-century chronicler named Szamoskoezy (just think what Smith might have done with a name like that!) wrote a description, hidden for centuries in manuscript form, which jibes exactly with Smith's description of the duels!

Having overcome the Hajdus, Sigismund attempted to get control of Transylvania. He was unable to do so, and most of his troops were slaughtered. John Smith related that he himself was left for dead on the field, restored to strength because he looked worth ransoming, and sold as a slave into Turkey. From there, his account continues, he was taken to the Crimea, and eventually escaped and got

A map from the 1627 edition of John Smith's Generall Historie of Virginia.

back to England. After a short rest he was ready to stretch his incredible luck by setting out for the New World.

"He could not possibly have written as he did about Hungary without having lived through the events he described," Dr. Striker has concluded. "It is time we gave him full credit for being not only a valiant fighter, but an acute historian and chronicler as well."

No one can claim that clearing Smith's name in southeastern Europe necessarily validates all he wrote about Virginia. But at least the reverse logic used so frequently by his detractors—If he lied so outlandishly about Hungary, how could he be trusted elsewhere?—applies. If he was so accurate and trustworthy in Hungary, isn't there reason to trust him in Virginia?

Quick to anger but quicker to forgive, bushy-bearded Captain Jack must be accepted for what he was—the last of the knights errant. Possessing no crafty, subtle mind, he acted first and pondered afterwards. If he had any philosophy, it was to meet problems as they came and make the most of every opportunity. This stepchild of Ulysses was never plagued with indecision or soul-searching. He never doubted, up to his dying day, that he could accomplish the impossible—perhaps because, on some occasions, he did. His pageantry and pretense were so incongruous in the vast wilderness that there is a Don Quixote-like pathos

about his story. If he had been fighting windmills and not Indians, we might find the whole thing quite amusing. John Gould Fletcher writes:

"He had displayed brilliant courage, but not deep wisdom; grappled for power, but not for the power that comes through a deep understanding of human limitations; seen strange seas, talked with strange people, and lived through an epic."

Americans who know nothing else about early American history can recount the dramatic tale of Smith's rescue on the block by the beautiful Indian princess Pocahontas. Whether or not Pocahontas really saved the gallant Captain at the execution block, and whether or not they were strongly attracted to each other, Pocahontas frequently visited Jamestown while Smith was there and stopped these visits after he had departed. We will never know just what the Captain meant when he called her the "nonpareil of Virginia." If he did not owe his life to her on that day in the forest, he did—in a historical sense—once he wrote about her years later.

Marshall Fishwick is associate professor of American studies at Washington and Lee University. He wrote "Sheaves of Golden Grain" for AMERICAN HERITAGE *(October, 1956). Among his recent books are* The Virginia Tradition *and* American Heroes: Myth and Reality.

READING, WRITING, AND HISTORY

What has been the impact of the American Civil War on the generations of novelists and poets since Appomattox? This subject is discussed below by Professor Daniel Aaron of the Department of English at Smith College, in place of the regular essay by Bruce Catton.

THE EPIC IS YET TO BE WRITTEN

Two years after Appomattox, William Dean Howells remarked that "our war has not only left us a burden of a tremendous national debt, but has laid upon our literature a charge under which it has hitherto staggered very lamely." According to an anonymous reviewer for *Scribner's Magazine*, it was staggering in 1904. "The war," the reviewer complained, "still waits for its novel, and will wait until . . . some man of genius shall steep himself in it and assimilate it." Despite the popular successes of *The Little Shepherd of Kingdom Come* by John Fox or Winston Churchill's *The Crisis*, the "epic character" of the war was an "easy commonplace in talk," but it was not "felt." It provided, he said, "a milieu full of color and possibilities," but it was also potentially boring for its beneficiaries of the next generation who suspected its idealism and who attributed its cause to a "variety of minor selfishnesses." The middle-aged writer of 1900—too young to have fought in the war and yet too close to see it as an epic—was incapable of reconstructing "the spirit of the last great struggle over an idea," but in time, he thought, such treatment would be possible.

But could a civil war "fought under modern conditions, and turning on such issues as negro slavery and the constitutional rights of secession" inspire an epic poem or a great novel? Was there "anything about the American conflict which would recommend it especially for poetic or literary handling"? Henry A. Beers, an English professor at Yale University who raised these questions in 1900, doubted whether any war later than the Crusades would "lend itself to epic treatment." The epic required distance, remoteness, legend, to give it the proper degree of enchantment. "A certain unfamiliarity," he declared, "is necessary for picturesque effect."

Feeling his way through masses of statistics, bulletins, and dispatches, the would-be epic poet of the Civil War was likely to lose himself in pedestrian details. He knew too much. He had to convert gun carriages and torpedoes into poetry and to evoke sublime thoughts about battles fought at such unromantic places as Bull Run, Pig's Point, Ball's Bluff, and Paddy's Run.

Beers, nevertheless, was not prepared to say categorically that the American Civil War would never lend itself to literary treatment. Unlike most wars, it was distinguished by "the grandeur of high convictions, and that emotional stress which finds its natural utterance in eloquence and song." In time, the poet and the romancer would fasten on the most dramatic episodes—Harpers Ferry, Gettysburg, the Andersonville prison, the death of Jackson, the duel of the ironclads, the assassination of Lincoln—and the lesser events would fade into the background.

Writing more than a half century ago, Beers commented perceptively (as Edmund Wilson was later to do) on the high literary merit of the non-belletristic Civil War memoirs, but he noted the failure of an American Scott or Tolstoi to emerge. Today it can still be said that no work of Civil War fiction has yet duplicated the blend of verisimilitude and emotion that makes the memoirs of Grant and Sherman, Mrs. Chesnut's diary, or Thomas Wentworth Higginson's *Army Life in a Black Regiment* so memorable. Indeed, it could be plausibly argued that this war, so obsessively studied, so minutely dissected, so brilliantly described, has not yet provoked a fictional work that we can confidently call a masterpiece.

Even as the war was being fought, the four writers probably best endowed to record it in history or fiction—Henry Adams, Henry James, William Dean Howells, and Mark Twain—never got close enough to it to observe it at first hand. Their unwillingness or incapacity to engage directly in the war (a fascinating problem in itself) cannot be attributed to their aloofness or apathy, nor does it mean that they failed to gauge its significance. It simply means that by avoiding the battlefields, hospitals, and camps, they disqualified themselves as reporters. For nineteenth-century accounts of the war itself, the fictional records of eyewitnesses or the stories and novels of writers for whom the war was a comparatively recent event, we must turn to men of different temperament and outlook: John W. DeForest, Ambrose Bierce, Stephen Crane, and Harold Frederic.

According to Howells, who tried without success to build up a following for DeForest, *Miss Ravenel's Conversion from Secession to Loyalty* (1867), DeForest's first novel, was the only work he had found that treated the war realistically and artistically. DeForest based the graphic war scenes of this novel on the letters he had sent home to his family during his three years' hitch with the 12th Connecticut Volunteers. In this novel he set down with bleak detachment a view of the war that masked little of its horror and barbarism. The scenes of carnage, the butcheries performed by the surgeons in the field hospitals, the episodes of cowardice, skulduggery, political favoritism, and bureaucratic bungling—the seamy side of the war corroborated in the letters of other eyewitnesses—are powerfully incorporated into *Miss Ravenel's Conversion*.

Graphic as a panorama of war, DeForest's book, in the words of Robert A. Lively, "was more a calamity in individual lives than a national experience," and this comment applies even more aptly to the brutal Civil War stories of Ambrose Bierce. Bierce transmuted his own very real war experiences (he had volunteered after Sumter and had fought in many actions) into a series of nightmares, and he took a sadistic pleasure in destroying his hapless soldiers. Like Henry Fleming in Stephen Crane's *The Red Badge of Courage*, Bierce's victims are tyrannized by their inner compulsions or broken by a destiny that is both impersonal and perverse. The incidents that Bierce and Crane describe might have occurred at Sevastopol or Sedan. What makes their work important in any account of Civil War literature is the deflationary influence they exerted on their successors—the serious ones, at any rate—who henceforth hardly dared to indulge in sentimental heroics.

The Red Badge of Courage is studded with unheroic phrases; it is deliberately antiheroic. Crane will write, for example: "There was a singular absence of heroic poses," or he will ironically observe that the "officers, at their intervals, neglected to stand in picturesque attitudes." In the conflagration of war, the human participants move like distracted ants, or Crane fuses them into mindless aggregates that bleed, reel back, disintegrate. Any soldier or officer who even tries to assert himself is ridiculed for his vainglory.

Just as the young writers of World War II fell unconsciously into the prose rhythms of Ernest Hemingway and adopted his attitudes, so many of the Civil War novelists projected the war, as Crane did, through the consciousness of a single bewildered hero and dwelt upon the chaos and indignity of war rather than on its glamour.

Harold Frederic, like Stephen Crane, was born too late to serve in the Union Army, but his fine novel, *The Copperhead* (1893), and his collection of war tales, *Marsena and Other Stories* (1894), have fallen into undeserved obscurity. The novel tells of the tribulations of an upstate New York farmer whose pro-Southern sympathies during the war bring upon him the concentrated hatred of his neighbors. The collection of stories focuses on this same community as well as on the war front and is notable for its sensitive recordings of casual events that probably occurred in small villages throughout the country during the war. He catches the anguished cry of a farmer when the first casualty lists come in:

"Wa'n't the rest of the North doin' anything at all?" a wild-eyed, disheveled old farmer cried out in a shaking, half-frenzied shriek from the press of the crowd round the telegraph office. "Do they think Dearborn County's got to suppress this whole damned rebellion single-handed?"

The successors of DeForest, Bierce, Crane, and Frederic scorn the painted dolls that once postured through the romantic tales of the eighties and nineties. The stench and muck of war have dispelled the odor of magnolia blossoms and roses; the splendid panoramas have faded, and the sociologists and the historians have taken over.

As fiction, many of these novels—James Boyd's *Marching On,* Clifford Dowdey's *Bugles Blow No More,* Allen Tate's *The Fathers,* Andrew Lytle's *The Long Night,* Stark Young's *So Red the Rose* come to mind—are of much higher quality than most of the early novels of the war. They are richer and denser and more reflective, and their authors are not inhibited by the taboos which bedeviled DeForest and Crane. The battle scenes in these novels are often extraordinarily realistic. But there is no mystery or awe in these books, little of that mythic sense without which the Civil War is likely to become a pastiche of gruesome or idyllic or merely commonplace details, or a historical background against which the novelist may project his social theories. The attitude I miss in the best of these modern Civil War novelists I find in Whitman and Melville, both of them romantic realists whose life and experiences and temperament made them such admirable reflectors and interpreters.

Whitman was heartened by the response of a nation to the "volcanic upheaval," but he saw it as a miracle, to be regarded with awe. *Specimen Days* and *Drum-Taps* are the "interior history" of the war that Whitman declared could never be written. He records the first response of the North to Fort Sumter: the contempt for the South, the mixture of anger, incredulity, and bravado, and the rout at Bull Run that leaves the country "baffled, humiliated, panic-struck." He mentions the courage of Lincoln on that "crucifixion day." He goes to Falmouth, Virginia, in December of 1862 and sees a cart-load of "amputated feet, legs, arms, hands." He sets down the acts of heroism and kindness performed by both sides, and the atrocious cruelties. Multiply these atrocities, he says

by scores, aye hundreds—verify it in all the forms that different circumstances, individuals, places, could afford—light it with every lurid passion, the wolf's, the lion's lapping thirst for blood—the passionate, boiling volcanoes of human revenge for comrades, brothers slain—with the light of burning farms, and heaps of smutting, smouldering black embers—and in the human heart everywhere black, worse embers—and you have an inkling of this war.

No one ever described more honestly than Whitman the dehumanizing effects of the Civil War: the released prisoners emerging into the light—a foreshadowing of Buchenwald and Auschwitz:

can these be *men*—these little livid brown, ash-streak'd, monkey-looking dwarfs?—are they really not mummied, dwindled corpses?

the toll of bullets, typhoid, dysentery, inflammations:

the dead, the dead, the dead, [he wails] *our* dead—or South or North, ours all, (all, all, all, finally dear to me).

Reading his poems and recollections, we believe him when he says, "I comprehended all, whoever came my way, northern or southern, and slighted none." And when he sees a portentous meaning in the tremendous storms of 1864 that seemed to trail the great battles of that year and the luminous nights as symbolic of the nobility that cuts through the "long stretches of murky gloom," he gives an epic proportion to a war that was not a "struggle of two distinct and separate peoples" but a conflict between "the passions and paradoxes" within a single nation.

This same Virgilian note is struck by Herman Melville in his seldom-read but profoundly moving volume of poems, *Battle-Pieces and Aspects of the War.* It opens with "The Portent," the image of a hanged John Brown swinging on the gallows, the beard streaming from beneath his death cap like a "meteor of the war," and it creates (to quote from Howells' review) "the unrest, the strangeness and solitude, to which the first sense of the great danger reduced all souls." Howells found Melville's poems, on the whole, too impalpable to be completely satisfactory, but he failed to see that Melville's reflective commentary on the course of the war from Bull Run to Appomattox served as a kind of Greek chorus to the national tragedy, that *Battle-Pieces* were the poetic notations of an observing but passionately engaged mind.

The tone of *Battle-Pieces* is one of mingled grief and irony. America, "the world's fairest hope," is linked with "man's foulest crime," and Satan, a "disciplined captain, gray in skill" has given the lie to American optimism. The ladies who cheer the young men marching off to war in "Bacchic glee" will soon learn to sorrow:

How should they dream that Death in a rosy clime
Would come to thin their shining throng?

Youthful veterans become prematurely old, like "The College Colonel" who quickly discovers that war is not a game:

A still rigidity and pale—
An Indian aloofness lines his brow;
He has lived a thousand years
Compressed in battle's pains and prayers.

Although he rejoices in Union victories, celebrates Gettysburg, the victory at Lookout Mountain, the capture of Fort Donelson, the exploits of individual heroes, his exultation is tempered with pity, and the spirit of his poetry is more elegiac than martial. A war which began with the vanities of plume and sash ends with swarms of "plaining ghosts" and the triumph of brute mechanic power.

Although he pronounces the supremacy of "plain mechanic power," Melville retains in *Battle-Pieces* the rhapsodic note, the romantic flourishes now deemed so inappropriate in any would-be realistic portrayal of the war. We have come to accept so completely the view that the Civil War was largely a record of tedium, vileness, and death that any attempt to write of it romantically, to deck it out with plumes and chargers, is dismissed as make-believe. Yet there is much evidence that many volunteers, in the early days of the war especially, were imbued with the most chivalric notions and that William Faulkner's dashing horsemen may be closer to their intended counterparts than the plain-talking soldiers of MacKinlay Kantor or James Boyd.

Listen to Charles Francis Adams, Jr., writing to his father in 1863:

In addition to the usual sights of battle I saw but one striking object—the body of a dead rebel by the road-side the attitude of which was wonderful. Tall, slim, athletic, with regular sharply chiseled features, he had fallen flat on his back, with one hand upraised as if striking, and with his long light hair flung back in heavy waves from his forehead. It was curious, no one seems to have passed that body without the same thought of admiration.

The most grimy accounts of the war in the letters and memoranda of eyewitnesses like DeForest, Adams, Oliver Wendell Holmes, Jr., or Sylvanus Cadwallader, contain similarly romantic interludes:

The Twelfth was still rocking back and forth [writes De-Forest in his war recollections—*A Volunteer's Adventure*] fluctuating between discipline and impulse, when an officer of Sheridan's staff (a dashing young fellow in embroidered blue shirt, with trousers tucked into his long boots) galloped into our front from the direction of Crook's column, and pointed to the wood with his drawn sabre. It was a superb picture of the equestrianism of battle; it was finer than any scene by Horace Vernet or Wouwerman. The whole regiment saw him and rejoiced in him; it flung orders to the winds and leaped out like a runaway horse. The wood was carried in the next minute. . . .

Young Holmes, fresh from Harvard, entered battle with the conviction that "high and dangerous action teaches us to believe as right beyond dispute things for which our doubting minds are slow to find words of proof." When wounded for the first time, his response was rehearsed and literary:

When I got to the bottom of the Bluff the ferry boat (the scow), had just started with a load—but there was a small

The Spectral Soldier

At last, they saw him stop and stand motionless. Hastening up, they perceived that his face wore an expression telling that he had at last found the place for which he had struggled. His spare figure was erect; his bloody hands were quietly at his side. He was waiting with patience for something that he had come to meet. He was at the rendezvous. They paused and stood, expectant. . . .

He was invaded by a creeping strangeness that slowly enveloped him. For a moment the tremor of his legs caused him to dance a sort of hideous hornpipe. His arms beat wildly about his head. . . .

His tall figure stretched itself to its full height. There was a slight rending sound. Then it began to swing forward, slow and straight, in the manner of a falling tree. A swift muscular contortion made the left shoulder strike the ground first.

The body seemed to bounce a little way from the earth. "God!" said the tattered soldier.

The youth had watched, spellbound . . . His face had been twisted into an expression of every agony he had imagined for his friend.

He now sprang to his feet and, going closer, gazed upon the pastelike face. The mouth was open and the teeth showed in a laugh.

As the flap of the blue jacket fell away from the body, he could see that the side looked as if it had been chewed by wolves.

The youth turned, with sudden, livid rage, toward the battlefield. He shook his fist. He seemed about to deliver a philippic.

"Hell—"

The red sun was pasted in the sky like a wafer.

—Stephen Crane, *The Red Badge of Courage*

boat there. Then, still in this half-conscious state, I heard somebody groan. Then I thought "Now wouldn't Sir Philip Sydney have that other feller put into the boat first?" But the question, as the form in which it occurred shows, came from a *mind* still bent on a becoming and consistent carrying out of its ideals of conduct—not from the unhesitating instinct of a still predominant & heroic *will*. I am not sure whether I propounded the question but I let myself be put aboard.

Even when Holmes had given up his convictions for a Hemingway-like military code, he found the faith "true and adorable which leads a soldier to throw away his life in obedience to a blindly accepted duty, in a cause which he little understands, in a plan of campaign of which he has no notion, under tactics of which he does not see the use." These superb young officers, these heroes who expose themselves to "Butternut" sharp-shooters, who ride with their long hair streaming behind, are not realistic to the "realists." But even if the average Johnny Reb was more likely to be (in the words of Charles Francis Adams, Jr.) "long, wiry, dirty, unshorn and dressed in the homespun yellow," the novelist or poet should not be automatically relegated to the "moonlight and honeysuckle school" because he invents a hero who resembles the romantic Confederate corpse that Adams saw by the roadside.

Only Faulkner, among the contemporary novelists, has created a myth about the Civil War. And even Faulkner's long saga of Yoknapatawpha County, which begins with a double crime—the introduction of Negro slavery and the private exploitation of a wilderness to which no person or group had just title—even Faulkner's microcosm only includes the war as an episode in a larger cosmic drama. Perhaps, as Whitman said, the story is too vast for any one book:

Of that many-threaded drama [he wrote] with its sudden and strange surprises, its confounding of prophecies, its moments of despair, the dread of foreign interference, the interminable campaigns, the bloody battles, the mighty and cumbrous and green armies, the drafts and bounties—the immense money expenditure, like a heavy-pouring constant rain—with, over the whole land, the last three years of the struggle, an unending, universal mourning—wail of women, parents, orphans—the marrow of the tragedy concentrated in those Army Hospitals—(it seem'd sometimes as if the whole interest of the land, North and South, was one vast central hospital, and all the rest of the affair but flanges) —those forming the untold and unwritten history of the war—infinitely greater (like life's) than the few scraps and distortions that are ever told or written. Think how much, and of importance, will be—how much, civic and military, has already been—buried in the grave, in eternal darkness.

And yet if historians (after spending years trying to illuminate this darkness) still disagree about the causes, consequences, and significance of the Civil War, why should we expect a revelation from the novelist or poet? It is really surprising that a people so attuned to the present and the future should not have taken the time to brood over the past? Did not the Civil War itself accelerate the momentum that transformed the nation in a few decades from a predominantly rural and decentralized society (where legend might slowly incubate) into an industrial urban society too new and noisy for retrospective contemplation? Is there any good reason, in short, why this war should have inspired a literary masterpiece?

Perhaps it would have been too much to expect some novelist in the triumphant North to dramatize the insight of Melville's "College Colonel" or the somber reflection of the Confederate vice-president, Alexander H. Stephens, brooding in the Charlestown prison. "There were barbarities, no doubt," Stephens wrote in his *Recollections,* "and atrocities on both sides horrible enough, if brought to light, to unnerve the stoutest heart and to cause the most cruel and vindictive to sigh over human depravity." The diffusion of such dark views might have shaken the nation's faith that Destiny (to paraphrase Emerson) had a sneaking fondness for it. It was safer to see the war as an accident, an aberration, a temporary disorder for which men, not Man, were responsible; it was more American to ignore its sinister import and to concentrate on the glittering future.

One might argue, of course, that the war is still too close to assess, that catastrophes of such magnitude cannot be imaginatively assimilated in less than a century. The Trojan War was long past before Homer interpreted it, and several hundred years separated Virgil and Shakespeare from the respective civil wars they commemorated. No great classic has ever been written about the English civil war of the seventeenth century, a struggle that offers parallels to our own. Thus far, only a few American writers, mystically attached to the Union, have felt the grandeur and the tragedy of the war and tried to construe an event that seemed to them at once personal and mythic.

The author of our as yet unwritten *Iliad* must do more than merely set down the experiences of a sickened and bewildered combatant if he is to capture the meaning of what Melville called "the great historic tragedy of our time." His hero may pick lice from his uniform, and ride with Jeb Stuart or Sheridan on a gaunt nag "with each rib visible and the hip-bones starting through the flesh." There may be "no pomp or pride" in his dilapidated hat. But he will not be untrue to history if he displays the "fierce friendship . . . appetite, rankness" and "superb strength" of Whitman's soldiers.

As the Civil War drops further and further behind the wake of history, it may acquire the legendary indefiniteness that will tempt the epic poet. Perhaps some unborn artist will then recapture the exultation and anguish of those extraordinary days when practical men were often mystics and when soldiers and politicians felt themselves to be actors in some preordained catastrophe.
—*Daniel Aaron*

116

One of the most talented Civil War propagandists was a citizen of Baltimore named Adalbert Johann Volck, a German emigrant who made his living as a dentist but who was a gifted artist and engraver. In 1861 he passionately espoused the Confederate cause —as did many others in Baltimore—and he created a remarkable series of etchings which had both high emotional voltage and genuine artistic excellence. He attacked the Union and its leaders, from Abraham Lincoln to Benjamin Butler (a favorite object of scorn in the South, which nicknamed him "Beast" Butler), and he extolled the Confederacy and its people. The sketches he did, their emotional power still undiminished, speak of the passion and heat of that terrible period when brother fought against brother and the nation struggled with itself for survival and unity. On these pages, some of the most striking of Volck's engravings are presented as a clue to the mystery of why embattled Southerners fought so long and with such effective fervor. We are indebted to Dr. W. B. Spinelli of Pittsburgh, Pennsylvania, from whose collection these etchings come, for permission to reproduce them.

—*Bruce Catton*

A Southern Artist on the Civil War

In the sketch at the top of this page, Volck bitterly caricatures Lincoln going through Baltimore on his way to his inauguration. A false rumor said Lincoln traveled in disguise; Volck takes a cruel advantage of it in this acidulous sketch. At left, Volck presents the supposed plight of New Orleans patriots, immured at Fort St. Philip by the heavy-handed General Butler, whom the South detested for his rule in occupied New Orleans.

Besides being a gifted strategist, General Stonewall Jackson was a devout Christian, and in his sketch of Jackson at a prayer meeting in the field, Volck displayed this side of him.

Citizens of Vicksburg, the Confederate stronghold in Mississippi, endured great hardships during the Federal siege. In

A Glorification of Southern Patriotism—

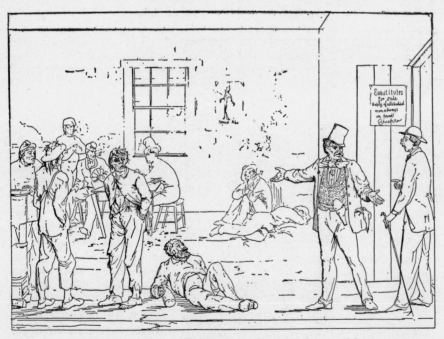

Scorn for the North was implicit in wartime cartoons. Here—without exaggerating too greatly—Volck excoriates the Northerners' search for substitute soldiers.

The Federals in occupied territory often were brutal in their search for

is sketch of a genteel southern
oman driven to a cave by the six-
eek Federal bombardment, Volck
peals to deep patriotic emotion.

Short of metals, the Confederates appeal to churches to turn in bronze bells for the casting of cannon. Here Volck shows an idealized concept of such a contribution.

Balanced by Depiction of Northern Cruelty

ncealed weapons. This cartoon dwells
n the ransacking of a southern home.

Moving armies left tragedy in their wake. Slightly overstressing the actuality of ruined homes, Volck captions this, eloquently, as showing Tracks of the Armies.

In the border areas war's horrors needed little embellishment. On the Missouri-Kansas frontier, Unionist "Jayhawkers" bore down hard on Southern sympathizers. Volck exaggerated slightly in this angry sketch.

Most hated of Union troops were the German-American regiments which served (among other places) in the Shenandoah Valley under Franz Sigel. Volck exploits antiforeign sentiment in attacking their looting.